Ground-breaking. Whatever your focus—
cing, sentencing, cyber-crime, interpersonal or state violence—this book
will change how you understand and interrogate technology and its role
in crime and justice. This book is not about the future; it is about the
now, and what will follow. It is rigorous, insightful, and exciting. It is
essential reading for scholars, students, and the general community: we
need to take up the challenge offered by this book.

Associate Professor Marie Segrave, Monash Unviersity, Australia

In *Crime and Punishment in the Future Internet* Sanja Milivojevic invites us
to look into the future and actively engage with digital frontier
technologies that, as she skilfully shows, bring risks as well as possibilities
into our lives. It as a brave and, above all, imaginative book that opens
important debates about the nature of crime and punishment that even
techno-sceptics and techno-phobes among us can no longer ignore. It
made me think—it still does—and this is all one can ask of a book.

Professor Katja Franko, University of Oslo, Norway

Crime and Punishment in the Future Internet is a remarkable achievement,
distilling complex technological concepts and criminological debates into
a concise, accessible, and highly thought-provoking text. As digitization
advances rapidly, Milivojevic's book will be essential reading for students
and scholars of Criminology seeking to understand emerging landscapes
of technology, crime, and control.

Professor Dean Wilson, University of Sussex, United Kingdom

CRIME AND PUNISHMENT IN THE FUTURE INTERNET

Crime and Punishment in the Future Internet is an examination of the development and impact of digital frontier technologies (DFTs) such as Artificial Intelligence, the Internet of things, autonomous mobile robots, and blockchain on offending, crime control, the criminal justice system, and the discipline of criminology. It poses criminological, legal, ethical, and policy questions linked to such development and anticipates the impact of DFTs on crime and offending. It forestalls their wide-ranging consequences, including the proliferation of new types of vulnerability, policing and other mechanisms of social control, and the threat of pervasive and intrusive surveillance.

Two key concerns lie at the heart of this volume. First, the book investigates the origins and development of emerging DFTs and their interactions with criminal behaviour, crime prevention, victimisation, and crime control. It also investigates the future advances and likely impact of such processes on a range of social actors: citizens, non-citizens, offenders, victims of crime, judiciary and law enforcement, media, NGOs. This book does not adopt technological determinism that suggests technology alone drives social development. Yet, while it is impossible to know where the emerging technologies are taking us, there is no doubt that DFTs will shape the way we engage with and experience criminal behaviour in the twenty-first century. As such, this book starts the conversation about a range of essential topics that this expansion brings to social sciences, and begins to decipher challenges we will be facing in the future.

An accessible and compelling read, this book will appeal to those engaged with criminology, sociology, politics, policymaking, and all those interested in the impact of DFTs on the criminal justice system.

Sanja Milivojevic is a Research Fellow in Criminology at La Trobe University, Melbourne, and Associate Director of Border Criminologies at Oxford University. Sanja's research interests include borders and mobility, security technologies and surveillance, gender and victimisation, and international criminal justice and human rights. She is a recipient of Australian and international research grants and was a NSW representative at the Australian and New Zealand Society of Criminology's Committee of Management (2012–2016). Sanja has been a visiting scholar at the University of Oxford, University of Oslo, Belgrade University, and University of Zagreb, as well as a Public Interest Law Fellow at Columbia University's Law School in New York. Sanja publishes in English and Serbian. Her latest book, *Border Policing and Security Technologies*, was published by Routledge (2019).

CRIME AND PUNISHMENT IN THE FUTURE INTERNET

Digital Frontier Technologies and Criminology in the Twenty-First Century

Sanja Milivojevic

Routledge
Taylor & Francis Group

LONDON AND NEW YORK

First published 2021
by Routledge
2 Park Square, Milton Park, Abingdon, Oxon OX14 4RN

and by Routledge
52 Vanderbilt Avenue, New York, NY 10017

Routledge is an imprint of the Taylor & Francis Group, an informa business

British Library Cataloguing-in-Publication Data
A catalogue record for this book is available from the British Library

Library of Congress Cataloging-in-Publication Data
Names: Milivojevic, Sanja, 1972- author.
Title: Crime and punishment in the future internet : digital frontier technologies and criminology in the twenty-first century / Sanja Milivojevic.
Description: Milton Park, Abingdon, Oxon ; New York, NY: Routledge, 2021. | Includes bibliographical references and index.
Identifiers: LCCN 2020050912 | ISBN 9780367467999 (hardback) | ISBN 9781003031215 (ebook)
Subjects: LCSH: Criminology--Forecasting. | Criminology--Technological innovations--History--21st century. | Criminology--Data processing--History--21st century.
Classification: LCC HV6025 .M538 2021 | DDC 364.0285--dc23
LC record available at https://lccn.loc.gov/2020050912

ISBN: 978-0-367-46799-9 (hbk)
ISBN: 978-0-367-46800-2 (pbk)
ISBN: 978-1-003-03121-5 (ebk)

Typeset in Bembo
by MPS Limited, Dehradun

CONTENTS

PREFACE

This book's subtitle could easily be *My love and hate relationship with precarious yet magnificent digital technologies*. It was early 2020. World affairs were looking grim, with static noise around impending pandemic clear to those who wanted to listen. I decided to buy a new iPhone 11 to cheer myself up. I was happy with my purchase until I tried the new virtual assistant Siri. Instead of a standard reply of 'good morning' or 'hello' to my 'Hey Siri', a male Siri voice replied with a casual 'uh-huh?'. To say that I was surprised and disappointed is an understatement. I spent days—if not weeks—trying to revert to a more 'conventional' Siri assistant, but to no avail. They all replied with a version of 'uh-huh', and there was nothing I could do about it. There was simply no way to avoid this rude Siri but to stop using the service altogether which, of course, I tried to do. Yet, every now and then, I give in and say 'Hey Siri' for a convenience of a quick answer, even though I know I will immediately get angry about the 'uh-huh' response.

Technology is so enmeshed into our lives and the above example proves how difficult it is to opt-out. The role technology plays in contemporary society is not limited to our comfort, health, business success, travel, and entertainment. Its ability to harm us or make decisions about our human rights and civil liberties is undisputable. Yet, there is very little literature on the intersections of crime and emerging technologies such as artificial intelligence or the Internet of things.

This book was written in lockdown during the 2020 COVID-19 pandemic and the process of writing it was cathartic and healing. Looking into the future is a good distraction from the present. Many people helped my thinking about our increasingly digital existence, either while having a coffee or as co-authors. They are (in no particular order): Marie Segrave (Monash University), Beth Radulski (La Trobe University), Mary Bosworth (Oxford University), and Leanne Weber (Monash University). Others are dear colleagues, on which intellectual tradition some arguments presented in this book have been built: Jude McCullough (Monash University), Dean Wilson (University of Sussex), Sharon Pickering (Monash University), Katja Franko (University of Oslo) and Emmeline Taylor (City, University of London). I would also like to acknowledge my dear friends and confindants who provided feedback for this volume, especially Michael Parry and Filip Orelj. Son, you are my beacon. I thank you all.

Thanks to Routledge and Tom Sutton for having faith in this project. After reading the book, please visit the book's companion website www.crimetechbook.com and continue the conversation. And finally, to my family: now you can call me a *bona fide* tech geek, not just a pretend one with dozens of gadgets.

LIST OF ABBREVIATIONS

AI	Artificial intelligence
AGI	Artificial general intelligence
ANT	Actor-Network Theory
AVs	Autonomous vehicles
CCTV	Closed-circuit television
DFT	Digital frontier technologies
DLT	Distributed Ledger Technology
DoS	Denial of Service
DDoS	Distributed Denial of Service
FBI	Federal Bureau of Investigations
FinTech	Financial Technology
ICT	Information and communication technology
IoT	Internet of things
IT	Information technology
NATO	The North Atlantic Treaty Organization
NGOs	Non-governmental organisations
OECD	Organisation for Economic Co-operation and Development
P2P	Peer-to-peer network
RDoS	Ransom Denial of Service
RFID	Radio Frequency Identification
SDGs	Sustainable Development Goals
STEM	Science, Technology, Engineering, Mathematics

STS	Science and technology studies
UAVs	Unmanned Aerial Vehicles
UK	United Kingdom
US	United States
US DARPA	US Defense Advanced Research Projects Agency
VALCRI	Visual Analytics for Sense-Making in Criminal Intelligence Analysis
WLAN	Wireless LAN network

1

INTRODUCTION

A journey into the Unknown

Imagine the following scenario: police officers arrive at a crime scene. There is a lifeless body on a pavement, and a 3D printed gun next to it. An officer approaches the gun and points an object to it. The two things connect. The object handled by an officer shows information about the gun: the date and place of printing, who printed it and from what materials, who bought it, and maybe even who handled/fired it. Alternatively, imagine this: a prospective terrorist goes to a hardware store to buy items they need to make a bomb. All the components they intend to buy have sensors that communicate with other objects, leaving a unique data trail. The smart things communicate this information to other smart things deployed by law enforcement who can now predict the likely outcome of this purchase. In the final scenario, think about this: prisons may soon become obsolete, thanks to the artificial intelligence (AI) and the Internet of things[1] (IoT) technology. A would-be terrorist's house from the previous scenario could serve as a prison cell: the front door would deny entry or exit if so ordered by the court of law. In the future, many objects, things and machines in our house, workplace, and public spaces—from doors, chairs, and beds to vehicles and planes—are likely to be connected through the IoT network and powered by AI. They will communicate with other things in the grid, record and monitor our behaviour, location, health, and mental state. They will move us from place to place and deliver our groceries. Critically, objects will also act on our behalf, potentially bypassing us in the process. They are likely to become smarter and increasingly independent, learning from and adapting to the environment and embedded algorithms.

While some of the above scenarios might not materialise, certain aspects of this futuristic hi-tech backdrop already exist. We are ever more fascinated with the advances of science and technology and their role in creating new possibilities for modern societies, as well as improving our well-being and experiences. Commentators argue that technology as 'the use of scientific knowledge to set procedures for performance in a reproducible manner' (Castells, 2004: 8) has the potential to 'completely modify the future course of the humanity' (Ghimire, 2018: 6). Indeed, as Howard (2015) suggests, behind every empire is a new technology. Navigating society in the desired direction requires the use, control, and oversight of the pace and trajectory of current and potential innovations. Imagining what might eventuate is essential even though it can be erroneous. Future, after all, is uncertain. Nevertheless, to prepare and make the right decisions, we need to look forward. The focus of our attention needs to be on all aspects of technology: objects (actual or virtual), activities, knowledge, modes of organisation and sociotechnical systems (Matthewman, 2011: 12), and in particular technological artefacts—the physical or digital products of scientific activities and knowledge.

The evolution of humankind has been a long and adventurous affair. A Swedish-American physicist and cosmologist, Max Tegmark (2017), suggests that life on Earth had three key stages, depending on life forms' ability to design itself. In Life 1.0 (a simple biological life), living creatures could survive and replicate. However, they could not evolve or design their biological hardware and software other than via a lengthy and painful process of evolution. Humans signify Life 2.0 (a cultural life), where software could be successfully designed (i.e. we can learn a foreign language or adapt to our surroundings by not eating peanuts if we are allergic). Nevertheless, we cannot alter our biological hardware (i.e. 'upgrade' our brains). As we move deeper into the twenty-first century, humankind is on the brink of Life 3.0 (a technological life), where intelligent life forms could design both its software and hardware. While we are yet (if ever) to see the birth of Artificial General Intelligence (AGI – 'strong' AI) that can understand, learn, and perform any intelligent task a human being can with no human input, smart devices powered by 'weak' AI are everywhere. Siri, Amazon Alexa, facial recognition software, Netflix viewing suggestions, and email spam filters are just some examples of our overwhelmingly technological reality. Be that as it may, we often reminisce on a failed hope that by now, innovations celebrated in decades of science fiction would become a reality: chatter regarding flying pods from *The Jetsons* are a frequent feature in our household. The driver behind this narrative is, aside from sci-fi movies and novels, the view predominant since the Enlightenment: that scientific and technological developments are the defining factor of progress. Techno-credulity—blind faith in technological solutions, as Lucia Zedner (2009) points out—is a hallmark of late modernity. We use our technological artefacts, such as smartphones, computers, and tablets, to read about medical breakthroughs, wearable and security technologies, AI and robotics, and many other endeavours in a range of disciplines, from medicine to physics, and from aeronautics to microbiology. As Kléber Ghimire (2018: 6) suggests, '[g]lancing at the current literature on future studies, one gets the impression that the future direction of humanity is all about technology'. When the outbreak of COVID-19 virus hit the world in 2020, many hailed technological innovations such as smartphone apps as critical tools needed to help stem the tide of the pandemic, monitor the spread of the disease, and facilitate treatment (HIMSS Media, 2020). Technology 'play[s] a crucial role in our collective attempt to make sense of the future' (Verschraegen and Vandermoere, 2017: 2), especially given the fact that the future is by default uncertain. As the future looks increasingly risky, even dangerous, we focus on technology and science, expecting miracles. Contagious diseases, the threat of global warming, expansion and potential use of weapons of mass destruction, mass shootings, and terrorist attacks are a constant in the media and public discourse, as we are seemingly only one step away from such disasters. The future seems precarious, as technology and science innovations emerge as indispensable tools that can tame the beast.

On the other hand, technology could be hazardous, if not fatal, for individuals, communities, or the humankind. As Matthewman (2011: 25) suggests, when we invent technology, we also invent the possibility of unwanted outcomes that the use of such technology. A growing network of modern Luddites call for restraint and, often, a dramatic rejection of new technologies.[2] In the future Internet of algorithms, AI, interconnected smart devices and autonomous machines (hereafter 'digital frontier technologies' – DFTs), unwanted outcomes of new technologies could be severe and global (see Bostrom and Cirkovic, 2011). The world's sharpest minds such as Stephen Hawking, Nick Bostrom, Yuval

Noah Harari, and Bill Joy warned about the potential impact of out-of-control technological developments to our future. The conclusion of many scholars in a range of disciplines is that, even seemingly benign technologies could be designed and developed to dominate (Matthewman, 2011: 6). As Harari (2018: 17) would have it, '[i]t is undoubtable … that the technological revolutions will gather momentum in the next few decades, and will confront humankind with the hardest trials we have ever encountered'. Every new technology, thus, 'invites its own sets of hopes and fears, raises as many questions as it answers, and resides in its own (false) binary between utopia and dystopia' (Papacharissi, 2019: Section 1; Introduction). I revisit this vital point throughout the book.

This chapter outlines some of the key themes explored in *Crime and Punishment in the Future Internet*, such as:

- The classification and overview of the DFTs and the rationale for their inclusion in the book;
- The significance of these technologies for crime prevention, offending, criminal justice responses, and penal policies.

This chapter also maps an overarching approach, as well as the aim and the structure of this volume.

Digital frontier technologies, society, and crime: A missing link

Above outlined radical transformation of contemporary societies, commonly dubbed the Fourth Industrial Revolution, has largely been underpinned by the development of emerging technologies. While there is no universal definition of frontier technologies, such technologies 'have the potential to disrupt the status quo, alter the way people live and work, rearrange value pools, and lead to entirely new products and services' (Manyika et al., 2013: 1). Frontier technologies are linked to the UN-defined Sustainable Development Goals (SDGs) as innovations that 'will reshape industry and communications and provide urgently needed solutions to global challenges', while having 'potential to displace existing processes' (Ramalingam et al., 2016: 16). These technologies are fast-changing, with significant political and cultural impact and economic value. They can improve humanity by, for example, eradicating hunger and contagious diseases, automating manual tasks, creating new and better-paid jobs, reducing carbon emissions, prolonging life expectancy, and improving the overall quality of life (United Nations, 2018: 1). The impact of such technologies is on the individual, social, and global level, as they improve people's lives, promote social prosperity, and protect the planet. Yet, we often do not know if the technology will be beneficial, detrimental, or both (and to what extent) until we see it used in an actual context (Matthewman, 2011).

A sub-section within frontier technologies are digital technologies that use algorithms or applications to perform tasks by generating, storing, or processing data. In 2016, the Organisation for Economic Co-operation and Development (OECD) classified digital emerging technologies as cloud computing, photonics and light technologies, blockchain, robotics, quantum computing, modelling simulation and gaming, grid computing, AI, IoT and big data analytics (OECD, 2016). This book focuses on four DFTs, defined as such by the United Nations (2018):

- Artificial intelligence and machine learning;
- The Internet of things ('ambient intelligence', 'smart devices');
- Autonomous mobile robots—autonomous vehicles and drones ('smart machines'); and
- Blockchain.

Most of the literature on the topic also identifies these technologies as leading or frontier (see, for example, Manyika et al., 2013; Briggs et al., 2019). Because of its size, this volume had to exclude some emerging DFTs such as quantum computing that is billions of times faster than an 'ordinary' computer, and as such can crack any encryption, including Internet banking, in seconds (Tvede, 2020). Pause for a second and think about the implications of this development for offending and crime control. I trust many upcoming volumes and research projects will engage with quantum computing and its social and criminological relevance.

Digital frontier technologies, thus, bring hope and risk. They constitute and modify people's behaviour, identities, status, and surroundings. Just think of your smartphone: how much did you adapt to this technology? How much did you change habits because of it? How quickly did addiction and adaptation to the technology develop? Critically, '[t]he affection we feel for our objects is greater than that which we feel for our fellow subjects' (Matthewman, 2011: 42). These technologies are also powerful actors and help create power relations. They are inseparable from us and form much of our existence. As Verbeek (2011: 29) would have it, '[o]ur reality is a web of relations between human and nonhuman entities that form ever-new realities on the basis of ever-new connections'. Yet, their impact on crime, offending, and victimisation has mostly been ignored. This book aims to fill this gap by examining the present and imagining the future, both hopeful and atrocious.

To do this is not an easy task. The book's title is *Crime and Punishment in the Future Internet* so by default, the book is aimed at criminological and legal audiences. In the book, I apply a traditional definition of crime as an activity that is defined as such in the law. While aware of the limitations of this definition, and while for most of my criminological career I applied the definition of crime that bypasses the narrow, legal definition to include the concept of harm, I have decided the legal definition should be applied in this book to ensure the clarity of the analysis. Although the volume uses mostly criminological lens, one cannot write such a book without dipping into the literature, theory, and knowledge in a range of disciplines: science and technology studies (STS), surveillance studies, political economy, philosophy, sociology, and policy studies, to name just a few. This volume needs to cast a wide net to analyse artefacts and their impact on crime and punishment. One needs to delve deep into disciplines that are not the author's area of expertise. Writing about mobile robots or blockchain is daunting for a person that, while early adopter of many technologies, has no expertise in these specific areas of academic inquiry. Indeed, for a criminologist, debating machine ethics or device communication in the IoT network is equally as unnerving. Therefore, I hope the reader will be both patient and sympathetic to (m)any shortcomings they find in the book, however obvious they might be. *Crime and Punishment in the Future Internet* is not aiming to capture all, nor most issues, vis-à-vis DFTs. It will also be modest in providing answers. This book is a *provocation*. Its primary and foremost purpose is to commence a dialogue—both in terms of critique and future research. I hope that, after reading the book, scholars in social sciences, humanities, science, technology, engineering, and mathematics (STEM), as well as the public, will join the debate to further our investigation of the digital frontier technologies-crime nexus.

Foresight approach, scanning and scenario writing

The central investigative and analytical tool applied in the book is the foresight approach used in STS, as a 'participative process in which evidence' on a particular topic or development 'is assessed, possibilities articulated, and actions proposed' (Miles et al., 2016: 4). The foresight approach has a long history. Like many other ground-breaking ideas, we can trace its origins to H. G. Wells, who maintained that there is a need for a systematic study of the future implications of new technologies:

> [Although] we have thousands and thousands of professors and hundreds of thousands of students of history working upon the records of the past, there is not a single person anywhere who makes a whole-time job of estimating the future consequences of new inventions and new devices. There is not a single Professor of Foresight in the world (cited in Miles, 2010: 1449).

The foresight approach in STS seeks to extrapolate, in an anticipatory and predictive manner, from emerging technological developments. Foresight builds on 'path dependency' (Matthewman, 2011) that looks at the history and current state of the technology, to conclude what the future might bring. As Matthewman (2011: 21) notes, to understand why our computer's keyboard does not start with 'ABCDE' but with 'QWERT', we need to look at the development of the typewriter. Foresight should lead to policy implications via a collaborative process. As Joseph Coates suggests, forecast 'is a process by which one comes to a fuller understanding of the forces shaping the long-term future which should be taken into account in policy formulation, planning and decision making' (Coates, 1985: 30). Thus, it involves three key elements: prospective analysis of long-term developments, policy applications, and participation of a vast pool of knowledgeable stakeholders (Miles et al., 2016). Foresight, thus, is not a prediction or forecasting; it is impossible to predict or foresee the future. One must remember the above-mentioned COVID-19 pandemic, and how much our world has changed because of it. No one could predict the outbreak of this disease in early 2020, although some entrepreneurs like Bill Gates came pretty close. Forecast, nevertheless, aspires to achieve precision. It aims to prepare and build resilience to what might come, however unpredictable and implausible it might be. The technological forecast is a complex and lengthy process of building up multiple pictures and creating visions of, but also influencing or shaping the developments of the future (Miles et al., 2016).

According to Popper (2008), the foresight approach includes five phases: pre-foresight, recruitment, generation, action, and renewal phase. In the pre-foresight phase, one needs to define the rationale and objectives of the project and design the methodology. In the recruitment phase, the research team and other participants are gathered. In the generation phase, the team should engage in an exploration of the key issues, trends and drivers, the impact on issues, trends and drivers on one another, and anticipate possible futures. Finally, in the action and renewal phase, innovation, change, and evaluation happen. This book utilises pre-foresight and generation phase vis-à-vis DFTs. It aims to scope technologies' current and likely impact on crime and punishment in the future (prospective analysis of long-term developments), explore the technology-crime nexus, integrate existing and create new knowledge, and provide visions and images of the future, with possible policy applications. The book aims to generate responses from a pool of knowledgeable stakeholders (I will elaborate on this strategy in Chapter 2), set the scene and prepare for the recruitment, action, and renewal phases of upcoming research projects in criminology and social sciences more broadly (participation element of foresight). It applies *scanning* and *scenario writing* as qualitative methods in foresight studies. Scanning 'involves observation, examination, monitoring and systemic description of the technological, socio-cultural, political, ecological and/or economic contexts' (Popper, 2008: 59). The approach applied here, thus, involves documenting and collating information via literature review, web search, policy, and bibliometric analysis of DFTs and crime intersections. Scenario writing, on the other hand, is 'the production of accounts of 'plausible' future events based on a creative combination of data, facts and hypotheses. This activity requires insightful and intuitive thinking about possible futures, normally based on a systematic analysis of the present' (Popper, 2008: 57). In the book, I adopt exploratory scenario writing that asks, 'what if this happens' questions: I look at possible developments in DFTs, analyse and hypothesise 'future history', and outline likely state of affairs (Miles et al., 2016: 128-129) pertinent to crime, offending, and crime control. The book, however, does not adopt a backcasting approach that defines a desirable future and work backwards to design steps and policies to achieve such a future. While backcasting is a critical phase in theorising crime and criminal justice in the future Internet, it should follow mapping the potential futures offered here. I revisit this point in the Conclusion.

This book does not seek to engage in fortune-telling or add to ever-growing crime-technology science fiction. It aims to start a conversation (and a joint scenario writing exercise) about current technological developments and their prospective expansions. The important point to make is that these technologies may or may not be as relevant as we predict them to be in the future. They might even fade into insignificance and/or disappear. Remember the Google Glass experiment? Deloitte suggested in 2014 that by 2015, millions of glasses will be sold to wearable-thirsty customers (Goodman, 2016), yet this never happened, and the project was put on the backburner. Many technologies, as Chase (2018) notes, never 'cross the chasm' (as people in marketing circles would say), and make it count. They never reach the threshold of having enough people to buy and use the product after it has been tested as a failure by early adopters, often merely because the technology was not fit for the purpose at that point in its development. Other innovations, however, come back as the technology improves, and find their application. We cannot know which technology is going to be relevant for criminologists and social scientists of the future. There are no assurances that a density of networked things will emerge or materialise on the timescale that is predicted, or that blockchain is going to be the next 'big bang'. If these developments do not occur as anticipated, much of the subsequent analysis about the social and criminological consequences will be off the mark. I offer some reflexive consideration of these limitations and risks throughout the book. But, if DFTs continue to develop as predicted, they are likely to have a significant impact on how we live and, importantly, how we engage with crime, victimisation, and punishment. Thus, we need to 'scan' them now, analyse their relevance, and identify the potential future trajectories and their implications, notwithstanding the fact that we really cannot know if and when such technologies will fully emerge to the extent predicted by experts, and what impact (if any) they might have on our lives and communities.

About the book

This book provides the first examination of crime and punishment in the future Internet. Given the scarcity of the literature on the topic, the book purports to offer an initial in-depth theoretical account of the expansion and impact of digital frontier technologies on offending, the criminal justice system, and the discipline of criminology. It strives to pose some criminological, legal, ethical, and policy questions linked to such development.

Crime and Punishment in the Future Internet aims to anticipate possible/probable impacts of DFTs on the micro and macro social level. It forestalls their wide-ranging consequences, including the proliferation of new types of vulnerability, policing and other mechanisms of social control, and the threat of pervasive and intrusive surveillance. Two key concerns lie at the heart of this volume. Firstly, the book investigates the origins and pathways of emerging digital technologies and their interactions with offending, victimisation, and criminal justice interventions. It also investigates the future advances and likely impact of such processes on a range of social actors: citizens, non-citizens, offenders, victims of crime, judiciary and law enforcement, media, and non-governmental organisations (NGOs). As I elaborate in the following chapter, this book does not adopt technological determinism that suggests technology alone drives social development (for more see Bunz and Meikle, 2018). It builds on Greengard (2015: xv), who noted that it is impossible to know where the emerging technologies are taking us. Yet, there is no doubt that DFTs will shape the way we engage with and experience criminal behaviour in the twenty-first century. As such, this book aims to start the conversation about a range of essential topics that this development brings to social sciences and to begin to decipher challenges we will be facing in the future. The words of George Monbiot (2017) ring so sincere right now: we need to act to own new technologies before they own us.

The overarching argument put forward in the following chapters can be broadly summarised as follows: for a long time, as Janet Chan (2018) reminds us, we have neglected the importance of things, whether they be algorithms, security devices, or walls that prevent people from crossing borders. We focused on humans and the impact we have on offending, victimisation, and crime control. With the rapid development of DFTs, we can no longer ignore their expansion and agency. Agency should not be conflated with intention. As Bunz and Meikle (2018: Section: Some agency, but no intention) suggest, 'technology has an effect, but no intention. It has agency, but does not follow an interest of its own'. At least not yet. What we might be witnessing, however, is a potentially seismic shift, a breakdown of existing techno-social fusions that have defined the humankind in the last 200 years. The rise of technology could accelerate the collapse of the thing-human alliance, while at the same time, the thing-thing alliance continues to grow. What becomes apparent is that humans are increasingly removed from decision-making, and we seem not to care. As Latour suggests, all agents in contemporary society should and do 'share the same shape-changing destiny' (Latour, 2014: 15). In the future Internet computer algorithms and smart devices/machines are likely to drive this change. They might become *the key actor*, while we—the humans—might find ourselves in the position to do the bidding for the key actor (see Michael, 2016). I suggest in the book that we need to rethink our role in the techno-social world of offending and victimisation and consider why it is essential we find our way back to the equation.

Outline of the book

Chapter 2 outlines the literature and central concerns and approaches adopted by this volume, recognising that there has been little critical engagement with the topic in social sciences. This chapter some theoretical frameworks adopted in the book (ubiquitous surveillance, preemption, Actor-Network Theory, automated policing, and justice), and offers a review of the literature in criminology, surveillance studies, STS, and other relevant social science and humanities disciplines. Chapter 2 also examines key themes critical for the book, such as surveillance, big data, security, and privacy in the age of smart cities and the future Internet.

Chapter 3 looks at the development of artificial intelligence and machine learning. AI has been in the focus of the scientific community since the 1950s. The commercial use of AI commenced in the 1990s; since then, machine learning has advanced to the point that 'systems are now capable of learning how to accomplish a task without having been provided with explicit steps for doing so' (United Nations, 2018: 33). Six years ago, Stephen Hawking hauntingly suggested that AI 'could spell the end of the human race' (Cellan-Jones, 2014). At the same time, AI has been singled out as a critical technology to support criminal justice interventions (Brahan et al., 1998). The chapter will explore the following key issues:

- The origins and developments of AI;
- AI, the law, and offending;
- Bias and error in AI: Automated crime profiling, predictive policing and 'crime forecasting'; and
- AI and the criminal justice system.

The Internet of things is poised to revolutionise the way we live and communicate and how we engage with our social and natural world. In it, objects such as household items, vending machines, and cars can sense and share data with other things, via wireless, Bluetooth, or Radio Frequency Identification (RFID) technology. Smart things are an example of persuasive technology (Verbeek, 2011) that can control their performance, but also our behaviour, experiences, and decisions.

Chapter 4 overviews recent developments in the IoT technology and their relevance for criminology. This chapter partially fills the gap in the literature, by flagging emerging issues criminologists and social scientists ought to engage with in the future. It serves, like the rest of the book, as a starting point in the conversation and invites scholars to engage in forecasting—if not preventing—the unwanted consequences of the IoT expansion.

Chapter 5 analyses the developments in the area of mobile robotics, in particular autonomous vehicles and drones. Driverless cars are poised to reduce traffic accidents, increase traffic efficiency, reduce pollution, and improve the quality of our lives in smart cities (Bonnefon et al., 2016). Drones have also been in the focus of the academic community for quite some time, especially in criminology and surveillance and border studies (Završnik, 2016). One of the fastest developing emerging technologies —autonomous mobile robots—raise a range of issues, such as their relationship with the law including the issue of ethical implications of their development and use, privacy, security, and the 'humanitarian' side of these technologies (for example, their use in border control and mobility management).

Chapter 6 offers an exploratory picture of the development and impact of blockchain and cryptocurrencies. In 2008, a person(s) under the name of Satoshi Nakamoto developed a revolutionary distributed ledger system that effectively replaced the trust in a government-backed institution by a trust in a computer code. Experts and governments, however, warned that 'criminals are using cryptocurrencies to facilitate crimes', and that 'blockchain technology may be able to play important roles in crime prevention and the transparency and accountability of processes and evidence management in the criminal justice system' (Kearns, 2018). This chapter seeks to explore the future of blockchain technology, whether and how this technology is changing offending practices, and blockchain's potential in preventing crime such as human trafficking and modern slavery. It also flags the importance of a merger of blockchain with other DFTs, especially when it comes to addressing some shortcomings and risks identified throughout the book.

Chapter 7 brings together key concerns and arguments presented in this volume. The chapter offers pathways for future engagement and research for academics, and possible course of action for advocates and policymakers. After reading the final chapter, please visit the book's companion website—www.crimetechbook.com, and continue the conversation.

Conclusion

Technology and its artefacts must be made more relevant to criminology. In the world obsessed with anticipation of events in order to prevent them from happening, digital technologies tasked to do just that flourish. This is just one reason why criminology of today must engage with emerging technologies as a matter of urgency. As social scientists, we are not well equipped or trained to understand where technologies are heading, and what this means for a range of social issues and relationships. We need a multidisciplinary team of experts in areas of technology, security, sociology, law, criminology—the list goes on—and we need to broaden our theoretical gaze. Importantly, we need to be proactive. As Howard (2015: xvii) reminds us, the IoT and frontier technologies might be 'a final chance to purposefully integrate new devices into institutional arrangements we might all like. Active civic engagement with the roll-out of the future Internet is the last best chance for an open society', the one where we remain active agents with (albeit limited) control and agency. This book is, thus, both timely and necessary, as it signifies the beginning of our engagement with DFTs in criminology and social sciences more broadly. It is a call to scholarly and social action for academics and advocates alike to foresee—if not prevent—potential injustices and 'collateral damage' of a breakdown in the human-technology nexus. Our journey starts with the theoretical overview of the field and relevant theories in criminology, sociology, and STS, and how they can assist in building a clearer picture of our technological future.

Notes

1 The Internet of things is a new technology, and its spelling differs. Variations of the spelling include the 'Internet of Things', 'Internet of things', and 'internet of things'. The Oxford English Dictionary spelling the Internet of things and an acronym the IoT will be used in this volume.
2 One such example is the destruction of 5G towers in the UK and the US in 2020 amidst fears they spread COVID-19. Satariano and Alba (2020).

References

Bonnefon, J.-F., Shariff, A., Rahwan, I., 2016. The social dilemma of autonomous vehicles. Science 352 (6293), 1573–1576.
Bostrom, N., Cirkovic, M., 2011. Global Catastrophic Risks. OUP Oxford, Oxford and New York.

Brahan, J.W., Lam, K.P., Chan, H., et al., 1998. AICAMS: Artificial intelligence crime analysis and management system. Knowl. Syst. 11 (5-6), 355–361.

Briggs, B., Buchholz, S., 2019. Deloitte Insights Tech Trends 2019: Beyond the digital frontier. Available at: https://www2.deloitte.com/content/dam/Deloitte/br/Documents/technology/DI_TechTrends2019.pdf.

Bunz, M., Meikle, G., 2018. The Internet of Things. Polity, Cambridge and Medford.

Castells, M., 2004. Informationalism, networks, and the network society: a theoretical blueprint. In: Castells, M. (Ed.), The Network Society: A Cross-Cultural Perspective. Edward Elgar, Cheltenham, United Kingdom Northampton, United States, pp. 3–45.

Cellan-Jones, R. 2014. Stephen Hawking warns artificial intelligence could end mankind. BBC News, 2 December.

Chan, J., 2018. Politics of the Anthropocene: Lessons for criminology. In: Holley, C., Shearing, C. (Eds.), Criminology and the Anthropocene. Routledge, London and New York.

Chase, C., 2018. Surviving AI. Three Cs, Bradford.

Coates, J., 1985. Foresight in federal government policy making. Future Res. Quart. 1, 29–53.

Ghimire, K., 2018. Future as an object of inquiry: an introduction. In: Ghimire, K. (Ed.), Future Courses of Human Societies: Critical Reflections from the Natural and Social Sciences. Routledge, Milton, United Kingdom, pp. 1–25.

Goodman, M., 2016. Future Crimes: Inside the Digital Underground and the Battle for Our Connected World. Anchor Books, New York.

Greengard, S., 2015. The Internet of Things. MIT Press, Cambridge and London.

Harari, Y.N., 2018. 21 Lessons for the 21st Century. Jonathan Cape, London.

HIMSS Media, 2020. Roundup: Tech's role in tracking, testing, treating COVID-19. Available from: https://www.mobihealthnews.com/news/roundup-techs-role-tracking-testing-treating-covid-19 (accessed 24.03.2020).

Howard, P., 2015. Pax Technica: How the Internet of Things May Set Us Free or Lock Us Up. Yale University Press, New Heaven and London.

Kearns I., 2018. Is Blockchain Good News or Bad when it Comes to Policing and Crime? Part 1. Available from: http://www.police-foundation.org.uk/2018/09/is-blockchain-good-news-or-bad-when-it-comes-to-policing-and-crime/ (accessed 3 July 2020).

Latour, B., 2014. Agency at the time of the Anthropocene. New Literary Hist. 45 (1), 1–18.

Manyika, J., Chui, M., Bughin, J., et al. 2013. Disruptive technologies: Advances that will transform life, business, and the global economy. Available at: https://www.mckinsey.com/~/media/McKinsey/Business%20Functions/McKinsey%20Digital/Our%20Insights/Disruptive%20technologies/MGI_Disruptive_technologies_Full_report_May2013.pdf.

Matthewman, S., 2011. Technology and Social Theory. Palgrave Macmillan, Basingstoke.

Michael, M., 2016. Actor-Network Theory: Trials, Trails and Translations. Sage, London, Thousand Oaks, New Delhi, Singapore.

Miles, I., 2010. The development of technology foresight: a review. Technol. Forecast. Soc. Change 77 (9), 1448–1456.

Miles, I., Saritas, O., Sokolov, A., 2016. Foresight for Science, Technology and Innovation. Springer, Cham, Switzerland.

Monbiot, G., 2017. Big data's power is terrifying. That could be good news for democracy. The Guardian, 6 March.

OECD, 2016. OECD Science, Technology and Innovation Outlook 2016. OECD Publishing, Paris.

Papacharissi, Z., 2019. Introduction. In: Papacharissi, Z. (Ed.), A Networked Self and Human Augmentics, Artificial Intelligence, Sentience. Routledge, London and New York.

Popper, R., 2008. Foresight methodology. In: Georghiou, L., Cassigena Harper, J., Keenan, M. et al. (Eds.), The Handbook of Technology Foresight: Concepts and Practice. Cheltenham, Edward Elgar, United Kingdom, Northampton, United States, pp. 44–88.

Ramalingam, B., Hernandez, K., Prieto Martin, P., et al., 2016. Ten Frontier Technologies for international development. Institute of Development Studies, Brighton, United Kingdom.

Satariano, A., Alba, D., 2020. Burning cell towers, out of baseless fear they spread the virus. The New York Times, 10 April.

Tegmark, M., 2017. Life 3.0: Being Human in the Age of Artificial Intelligence. Penguin Books Limited, United Kingdom.

Tvede, L., 2020. Supertrends: 50 Things You Need to Know about the Future. John Wiley & Sons, Incorporated, Newark.

United Nations, 2018. World Economic and Social Survey 2018: Frontier technologies for sustainable development. United Nations Department of Economic and Social Affairs, New York.

Verbeek, P.-P., 2011. Moralizing Technology: Understanding and Designing the Morality of Things. University of Chicago Press, Chicago, United States.

Verschraegen, G., Vandermoere, F., 2017. Introduction: shaping the future through imaginaries of science, technology and society. In: Verschraegen, G., Vandermoere, F., Braeckmans, L. et al. (Eds.), Imagined Futures in Science, Technology and Society. Routledge, London and New York, pp. 1–12.

Završnik, A., 2016. Drones and Unmanned Aerial Systems: Legal and Social Implications for Security and Surveillance. Springer, Cham, Heildelberg, New York, Dordrecht, London.

Zedner, L., 2009. Epilogue: the inescapable insecurity of security technologies? Aas, K.F., Gundus, H., Lomell, H. (Eds.), Technologies of InSecurity: The Surveillance of Everyday Life. Routledge, Abingdon and New York.

2

BIG DATA, SECURITY, SURVEILLANCE, AND THEORISING THE FUTURE INTERNET

Introduction

Technology defines contemporary societies. Yet, the role of digital frontier technologies and how they shape our future—in particular, crime and offending—is little understood and even less theorised. Criminology is not an exception to this rule. As Hayward and Maas (2020: 2) note, for too long '[n]ot only [did] most criminologists ignore matters relating to technology itself, but … have shown a studied disregard of theories from other disciplines that have sought to open a space for dialogue between social sciences and information and communication technology'. Criminological gaze during the Fourth Industrial Revolution mostly focused on cyber-crime, hacking, surveillance, and digital fraud (Leman-Langlois, 2008; McGuire, 2012; Goodman, 2016; Powell et al., 2018).

This chapter outlines the central conceptual concerns and approaches adopted by this volume. The chapter first examines phenomena that are the precondition and/or the outcome of the application of DFTs in the future Internet, such as big data, surveillance, security, and privacy. Outlining and analysing these themes are essential if we wish to look at the impact of the IoT, blockchain, or autonomous mobile robots on future crimes, victimisation, and social control. To understand the role and impact of the IoT, for example, we first need to investigate the extent and types of surveillance this technology generates, and what this means for the privacy of users/consumers and those who decide (or manage) to ignore the temptation of smart things. The chapter also offers a review of relevant literature in criminology, surveillance studies, STS, and other social science and humanities disciplines vis-à-vis big data, surveillance, security, and privacy.

In the second part of the chapter, I outline theoretical approaches used in analysing and forecasting crime and punishment in the future Internet, in particular Actor-Network Theory (ANT), ubiquitous surveillance, technological unconscious, pre-emption and pre-crime, and predictive policing and automated justice. Rather than outlining them in-depth, the chapter will provide a brief introduction to the selected theoretical approaches as they will be discussed in greater detail throughout the book.

The themes underpinning, enabling, and ensuing digital frontier technologies

In discussing AI, the IoT, distributed ledger technologies, and autonomous mobile robots, some common grounds begin to emerge. First, these technologies seem to be in a permanent state of transition and flux. As will be explored in the following chapters, the scale of development and progress is astounding, often described as exponential. These technologies also leave a digital trail by generating, storing, and exchanging data about their activity, us, and the environment. They are things, machines, or software applications that sense and exchange, collaborate, verify, and act, based on data, sometimes without our knowledge or input. Digital frontier technologies also raise concerns about (personal, community, national, border) security. Its users face implications pertinent to their privacy, but other actors who did not agree to technology's 'terms and conditions' are also affected by it: bystanders, passengers, buyers, and sellers. We start by unpacking a complex phenomenon of big data.

Big data: The new oil?

An enormous amount of data is generated in our micro-universe every single day. From the moment we wake up and even as we sleep, a range of artefacts constantly observe, store, exchange, and analyse data about us and our activities. Data is a backlog, a history of our existence—and the one that we, at times, cannot erase. Often, we are unaware of the process of data creation. A computer logs in cookies every time you use it without you knowing what happens under the bonnet; smart toothbrush collects and stores data about your cleaning practice every time you turn it on; your car records data about travel and the health of the car. Examples mentioned above are what Rob Kitchin (2014) calls 'automated' processes of generating big data, in which records are created autonomously, without our interference. On top of this, we also 'volunteer' data by using social media platforms or loyalty cards. The third method of generating and collecting big data is directed—when human agents or organisations obtain data via, for example, public closed-circuit television (CCTV) systems. Once collected, a range of actors receive data about us and our activities: software developers, companies that own the product we wear or use, advertisers, banks, doctors, police, the government, and the list goes on. Notably, big data 'appear to offer answers to a wide array of problems of (in)security by promising insights into unknown futures' (Aradau and Blanke, 2017: 1). As such, commentators and stakeholders see big data as a tool that can help pre-empt future crimes. By examining data we analyse today but focus on the future. However, as I suggest later, 'a lot can go wrong, when we put blind faith in big data' (O'Neill, 2017: 2:11).

Definitions of big data often include 'three Vs': a *volume* of data, the increased *velocity*, and *variety* of collected data (Bennett Moses and Chan, 2014; Chan and Bennett Moses, 2016). Some authors add more Vs to the mix: veracity, value, and vulnerability (Završnik, 2018). The power embedded in having access and control of big data is so immense that in 2006, the British mathematician Clive Humby (cited in Wall, 2018: 29) suggested that big data is the new oil. Similarity does not stop there: big data, like oil, cannot be used until refined. Data need to be analysed and transformed into a product that can be used for a variety of purposes: from predicting consumers' behaviour and advertising products and services, to crime forecasting. Giving meaning to datasets transforms data to information generating a more comprehensive picture of the phenomenon that is structured and arranged in a particular context and provides knowledge (Kitchin, 2014; Lupton, 2014). Big data, thus, also refers to the process of using data more productively and profitably (Cale et al., 2020) via data mining—extracting patterns from large datasets. Put simply, data mining or 'data crunching' is making sense of data and using information in the most effective (or lucrative) way. Still, as boyd and Crawford (2012: 662-663) suggest, there is another essential element that defines big data (with technology and analysis): it is mythology as 'the widespread belief that large data sets offer a higher form of intelligence and knowledge that can generate insights that were previously impossible, with the aura of truth, objectivity and accuracy'. This often-criticised notion that algorithmic decision-making is both omnipotent and bias-free will be explored at length in the following chapters.

In 2020, data-linkage as the process in which big data informs policy (Cale et al., 2020) is a standard practice across the globe. During the outbreak of COVID-19, for example, big data was at the epicentre of efforts to comprehend and forecast the impact of the virus, identify the carriers and infected persons, and determine the best practice in containing the disease (Bean and CIO Network, 2020). In the criminal justice system, big data has seen an application in crime prevention, surveillance, and prediction of the likelihood of offending and recidivism (Cale et al., 2020). The role of big data is so significant that it has changed the terminology in almost all areas of criminological engagement with crime and punishment; crime-relevant knowledge is now routinely dubbed as databases, reasoning equals algorithms, crime prevention and investigation is called predictive policing, while criminal prosecutions became examples of automated justice (Završnik, 2018). Big data also serves to promote specific political and financial interests: 'doing more with less' and getting more money for it is the bottom line for its use (Završnik, 2018). The monetisation of our data and data about us is critical in the development of digital frontier technologies. However, this aspect of DFTs, while briefly mentioned, will not be the focus of the attention in this volume (for an overview of the literature and key themes see Powell et al., 2018).

Critically, most of us do not understand big data: how it works, or the algorithms used to process it. Creating strategies and the ability to see through what Lyon (2015) calls 'techno fog' is an essential feature of this book. As I will demonstrate in the following chapters, in the future Internet the expansion and application of big data brings a concern that decisions about crime and responses to offending are likely to be non-transparent, and beyond our scrutiny. The prospect that such decisions might not be in the hands of human experts only complicate the matter. Decisions about our likelihood to commit a crime in the future, criminal accountability, sentencing, parole, and bail might be based on patterns identified via big data and performed and executed by algorithms.

Security and risk: Inventing the future

The second theme that underpins both the development and deployment of digital frontier technologies is security and risk. In the twenty-first century, pursuing security and anticipating, preventing, and managing risk have become a priority in all aspects of modern life, including formal social control. Long neglected in criminology (Huysmans, 2006; Zedner, 2009), security has recently emerged as a critical theme in analysing offending, victimisation, and the criminal justice responses (Zedner, 2009; Bigo, 2016). This rediscovery of security happened alongside a conceptual change, as security ceased to be seen as safeguarding nation-state against foreign invaders, a narrative predominant during the Cold War. Security was widened and tied to the notion of survival: of an individual, community or a group, a nation state, and the humankind. Security has also infiltrated criminal justice, as strategies to prevent risks emerged as justification for repressive and punitive crime and social control policies (McCulloch and Wilson, 2015). Risks—local, national, global—seem to be multiplying. Migration, climate change, technology, economic concerns, biodiversity loss, weapons of mass destruction, pandemics, and cyber-crimes are ongoing, fluid threats that require intervention and management. The popularity of security/risk framework in current public policy is largely the outcome of 'security framing' and 'the creation of a continuum of threats and general unease in which many different actors exchange their fears and beliefs in the process of making a risky and dangerous society' (Bigo, 2002: 63). Risk is both real and constructed. Mobility and asylum, for example, are relatively recent additions to the pool of threats to the nation (Bigo, 2002; Huysmans, 2006; Milivojevic, 2019), and not because there was an increase in illegalised migration or asylum claims; it was politically motivated and executed project across the Global North.

There are many securities in contemporary society: political, military, economic, social, health, individual, national, international, existential, technological, border security. They are pursued by a range of government and non-government actors, often with little compromise and through the process of securitisation (Wæver, 1995). Undoubtedly, as Huysmans (2006) note, there is a hierarchy among securities, as national security claims have recently been trumping human security. Security itself, however, is not an end goal of this process, as it is likely unattainable. It is the pursuit of security that matters. In it, 'things that would ordinarily be politically untenable become thinkable' (Zedner, 2009: Section The semantics of security). Tackling crime is not an exception. Predictions whether someone is going to commit a crime in the future have long been a part of the criminal justice stratagems. However, as it will be explored later in the book, managing risk through crime prevention is losing ground to tackling uncertain risks. Such interventions do not require any evidence of a threat. It is *given* that such a threat exists.

In an era of big data, technology has been singled out as a critical tool that could identify, but also the tool that carries risk. During the COVID-19 global pandemic, we witnessed the rise of technological and other measures brought to combat the virus (Walker, 2020). We have also seen a conversion of the whole groups of people from 'responsible' to 'conditional' citizens (Zedner, 2010) according to how they responded to technologically-mediated risk[1]. On the other hand, as Beck and Willms (2004) suggest, in the second modernity where juxtaposing trends such as individualisation and globalisation are the hallmark, many perceive digital frontier technologies as potential global catastrophic risks (Bostrom and Cirkovic, 2011). Technology and its development are increasingly becoming a major source of social anxiety (Matthewman, 2011: 26).

Both accounts around technology—techno-credulity and technology as risk—are prominent in debating crime and responses to offending. Technology, as commonly argued by law enforcement and security professionals, could assist us in deploying early interventions via criminal justice actors and other government agencies before the commission of crime occurs. Reliance on technology-driven risk assessments rests on the logic of risk management that sees threats (in this case crime and (re) offending) as calculable and predictable, risky populations or individuals as identifiable through bias-free processes, and data as reliable and objective (Zedner, 2009). Hence, paramount protection against future terrorist attacks are artefacts such as hi-tech body scans. As I suggest in the following chapters, this narrative is quickly expanding with the development of DFTs. The IoT, AI, blockchain, and autonomous mobile robots are marketed as security paraphernalia that aim to make our lives more comfortable and as risk-free as possible. An AI-powered driverless car, it is reasoned, is much safer than any human-driven ones. Your smart chair will prevent any future health problems by sending data about your weight and posture to a doctor, who is going to prescribe diet and medication and prevent a potential heart attack. Cryptocurrency usage is going to protect you from online fraud and double spending. Importantly, emerging technologies will pre-empt crime before it happens by identifying where it might happen and who is likely to commit it. Smart machines and devices are and will continue to be used in criminal courts to 'predict' a likelihood of recidivism, and in assessing bail and parole applications, potentially removing humans from the decision-making process. This important theme will be explored in detail throughout the book.

Surveillance and privacy

There is, it is often contended, a price to pay to achieve this risk-free, crime-free, security-laden world: our privacy, one of the fundamental rights and civil liberty that belongs to all humans. It is a necessary trade-off, as commentators and politicians remind us, if we are to prevent future harms (see Finn and Wright, 2012; Powell et al., 2018). In the case study of COVID-19 pandemic, online monitoring and tracking of the population was deemed necessary to prevent new outbreaks of the virus (HIMSS Media, 2020; Bean and CIO Network, 2020; Walker, 2020). The same logic applies to crime; we should be watched and monitored to be safe. After all, if you have nothing to hide, you have nothing to fear.[2] The utilitarian motto of the greater good for the majority is driving mass surveillance practices we see today. The digital era's undisputable fact is that 'we are living in a time when more information is gathered, collected, sorted, and stored about the everyday activities of more people in the world than at any other time in human history' (Andrejevic, 2012: 91). DFTs greatly augment surveillance as the 'focused, systematic and routine attention to personal details for the purpose of influence, management, protection or direction' (Lyon, 2007: 14). A considerable proportion of contemporary surveillance is automated or volunteered. Our phones, computers, digital assistants, fitness trackers, and other smart things automatically observe and monitor our activities, habits, daily routines, where we shop, what gym we go to and for how long, and the list goes on. Many devices and machines that surround us continuously collect and share information about who we are and what we do. In addition, we often willingly share information about us on social media platforms, by using loyalty cards and ticking the Terms and Conditions box when downloading new software to our computer or smartphone.

While most of this surveillance appears to be *non-strategic*—a routine, auto-pilot attendance to a person or factors associated with a person—it often involves a conscious strategy to gather information about subjects of surveillance (Marx, 2012). Contemporary surveillance spills across the society, 'jolted' by "security demands" and technology companies' relentless marketing (Bauman and Lyon, 2013). Surveillance is no longer fixed and solid but liquid, reaching areas of social life where its presence was not prominent until now. Our lives are becoming increasingly transparent to employers, corporations, national and foreign government agencies, and other actors that have access to data. While our habits, relationships and actions grow visible, those that have access to data become increasingly invisible to us (Lyon, 2015), and so does the technology that enables it.

In the new world of big data, privacy is experiencing a major transformation. Poster argues that this has resulted in a super-panopticon, an ultimate version of Bentham's and Foucault's omni-seeing society[3], 'a system of surveillance without walls, windows, towers, or guards' (Poster, 1990: 93). While this theoretical framework is arguably not applicable to contemporary digital society for reasons I will elaborate on later in the book, the development and use of emerging technologies is likely to augment this issue. Surveillance and privacy are set to experience even bigger makeover in years to come. Importantly, we are likely to give our privacy away. We will be *obedient* to a new 'surveillant assemblage' (Haggerty and Ericson, 2000) of DFTs—a growing network of heterogeneous smart things, databases, algorithms, and knowledge. This network will uncover us (or as Haggerty and Ericson suggest, our 'data doubles') to those who listen. Critically, the above process of breaking down the human is just the beginning.

Theorising crime and punishment in the future Internet

In a digital world, technology is continuously transforming, impacting on, and being impacted by societal forces. Mobile phones were once devices used for phone calls or texts. Today, they are small computers, compact yet so powerful that a smartphone charger has more processing power than the computer that sent humans to the Moon in the 1960s (Porter, 2020). Modern technology is so complex that we often struggle to comprehend it. How many of us understand the ability to find someone in a crowd, via facial recognition cameras, in a matter of seconds? Do we really know how self-driving cars or bitcoin works? For Jacques Derrida, this lack of comprehension is one of the leading causes of today's existential struggles (see Matthewman, 2011: 23). Theorising technology, thus, is a challenging task.

Matthewman (2011) suggests there are three broad schools of thought in examining technology in the social context: technological determinism or the anti-humanist approach, humanist approach or social constructivism, and finally, the post-humanist approach. Technological determinism suggests that technology drives the development of the humankind and is the decisive force in that development. Technology is by nature removed from the society; it is autonomous, a-social. It exists in a given form because it must, as it is rational and inevitable in such form—there is a linear trajectory in the development of technology, from a steam machine to AI. The humanist approach, as its name suggests, places humans as critical actors in this development. Society, or at least some of its elements, is embedded in technology. Technology exists in a specific form because humans created and modified it. One of the most used examples for the humanist approach is the development of a bicycle: it was because of the demand for safety that large-front-wheel velocipedes were replaced by bicycles we use today. Post-humanism maintains that agency is distributed among all the actors in the process, not just technology or just humans. Society is configured from a range of technology-social assemblages, and both humans and non-humans have agency and can create actions (see Matthewman, 2011: 15–19). This book embraces post-humanism, in the sense that it considers both humans and non-humans as critical agents when it comes to the development and impact of DFTs in the future Internet. The approach applied in the following chapters is one of a relative symmetry: the focus is on humans, non-humans, and notably, on human-non-human connections. Humans and technology have co-agency in contemporary society and actively shape one another's development: emerging digital technologies shape humanity, and society shapes them in reverse. Our smartphones, for example, changed our morning routine as the phone is often the first thing that we look at when we wake up. What this book is interested in, however, is whether we are potentially on our way out of this equation. The question I pose in the following chapters is whether the development of AI, the IoT, mobile robots, and blockchain—in the broader social milieu of big data and surveillance—is going to disturb the equilibrium between humans and DFTs to the point that our agency diminishes, while the technology's impact on our lives, health, and importantly, offending, victimisation, and punishment continues to grow?

While many theoretical frameworks that apply to technology more generally could be used to explain the development and impact of DFTs, others fall short in this quest. This chapter provides an overview of theoretical frameworks from a range of disciplines—STS, criminology, sociology—applied in the book. This list is certainly not definitive; I am sure there are many theories the reader was hoping to find here that were not included. The reason is simple: this volume is the starting point in the conversation, rather than a complete guide to crime and responses to offending in the future Internet. And as every starting point, it includes a range of pertinent theoretical approaches identified across the above disciplinary fields.

Actor-Network Theory and technology as companion species

Actor-Network Theory is commonly used to explain the role of artefacts in social settings, and as such, is a potentially useful framework to analyse technology-crime nexus (although the theory was not designed or intended for this purpose). Created by Bruno Latour, Michel Callon, and John Law in the early 1980s, and while not a theory in the classical sense, ANT has been applied to a range of domains and contexts, from medicine to IT[4]. The actor in ANT is a source of action, regardless of whether the actor is human or non-human. Human and non-human elements are continuously combined in various assemblages—*hybrids*—and should be analysed as such. The key premise of ANT is the importance of non-human actors occasionally called actants as this terminology rejects an anthropocentric meaning attached to the concept of an actor[5]. As Latour (1996: 373) would have it,

> [a]n actor in ANT is a semiotic definition – an actant – that is something that acts or to which activity is granted by another ... an actant can literally be anything provided it is granted to be the source of action.

Non-humans, thus, are critical to actions and reactions in the social context, in combination with other actors and in a particular setting; humans and non-humans are relational (Michael, 2016). The social is heterogeneous; power, knowledge, and action are embedded and performed by many forms (Matthewman, 2011: 104), including non-humans. ANT claims that actants have a 'variable geometry': it is impossible to determine in advance which elements of the network are going to produce 'an agency effect' and action in the social context (Blok and Jensen, 2011).

In *the Pasteurization of France* and later works, Bruno Latour suggested that many actors caused scientific discoveries of French chemist and microbiologist Louis Pasteur. It was because of medical professionals, sceptics, researchers holding other theories, health administrators, city planners, scientific instruments and, of course, the microbes and pathogens themselves that Pasteur managed to discover the principles of vaccination, fermentation, and pasteurisation (see also Blok and Jensen, 2011). Non-human actors such as bacteria, scallops, or trees come from the natural world or are human-made, such as walls and buildings. They play a critical role in the advancement of actions, power, and scientific knowledge as they change the course of social events and create interference. Latour (1999: 179) memorably commented that '[y]ou are a different person with a gun in your hand'. Therefore, people don't kill people; guns don't kill people; but people with guns do kill people (Matthewman, 2011: 118; see also Michael, 2016). Non-human actors have full agency and are intrinsically connected to humans creating hybrids. The outcome of such connection is 'the simultaneous production of knowledge and construction of network of relationships in which social and natural entities mutually control who they are and what they want' (Callon, 1986: 59). Importantly, human and non-human elements are on the same level of importance (Lezaun, 2017).

Two types of entities exist in networks: intermediaries and mediators. Intermediaries 'transport meaning or force without transformation: defining its inputs is enough to define its outputs'. Mediators' input, on the other hand, does not translate into the defined output. They 'transform, translate, distort, and modify the meaning of the elements they are supposed to carry' (Latour, 2005: 39). Intermediaries reproduce associations. Mediators can make something happen that is not necessarily an outcome of what is set in motion by actors/actant in the network. Mediators, thus, transfigure and deform the message passed between entities in the network; they can disrupt, but also proliferate and complicate associations (Michael, 2016). As it will be demonstrated later in the book, the development of DFTs results in many mediators and hybrids that continuously alter the social fabric and relationships. They have relationships with one another of a sort that they make others do, sometimes unexpected, things (Latour, 2005: 106). Networked AI, the IoT, and mobile robots cooperate to reach common goals which may or may not align with the goals set by humans when programming 'smart things'. In the following chapters, ANT will be used to explain the impact of technology-human hybrids on crime and responses to offending. Their growing networks will be explored, as well as the role of humans in the thing-human alliance of the future. Importantly for our analysis, as technology progresses, so does its non-transparency. We simply focus on inputs and outputs, not on the technology's internal complexity. Technology becomes imperceptible, part of the background, and we accept it as such, without questioning its operations, ethics, and impact. Latour (1999: 304) focuses on this process of *blackboxing* as the process in which 'scientific and technical work is made invisible by its own success'. What is in black box no longer needs to be considered and cannot be problematised (Michael, 2016); inputs and outputs are the only points we need to discern. I will revisit this important point later on.

Related to ANT and applicable to emerging digital technologies are concepts developed by Donna Haraway and Deborah Lupton. Haraway's seminal work on the figure of cyborg suggests that humans and non-humans cannot be conceptually detached (Haraway et al., 1995). She uses the term 'companion species' to describe the cohabitation and co-evolution of humans, animals, and technological artefacts (Haraway and Wolfe, 2016). Lupton furthers these ideas by analysing our connection to mobile phones and wearable devices that effectively create 'human–data assemblages' (Lupton, 2018), somewhat akin to ANT's hybrids. Just as data learn from us through information about us, our habits, and activities, we also learn from data we get back from technology and adjust our lives accordingly (Lupton, 2016; Lupton, 2018). Analysis of this symbiosis and mutual dependency is going to be a critical theoretical hook in this volume. Importantly, as Lupton (2016: 3) suggests, '[w]e may begin to think about our digital data assemblages as companion species that have a life of their own that is beyond our complete control'.

Ubiquitous surveillance

In the contemporary world, surveillance is not merely post-panoptical (Bauman, 2000): it is ubiquitous (Lyon, 2007; Andrejevic, 2012). To be 'off-grid' today, one needs to go to great lengths, often with limited success. CCTV networks in the UK capture every step citizens make (Taylor, 2010), while some commentators dub China a 'surveillance state' (Qiang, 2019). A powerful example of just how difficult it is to avoid it is a reality TV social experiment called *Hunted* aired on UK's Channel 4 since 2015. We watch and often cheer for desperate contestants who try in vain to evade dedicated trackers who, often with ease, manage to locate and 'hunt' them down. As the head of the *Hunted* taskforce noted, '[a] typical fugitive hunt will begin with some basic details [about the hunted], but within hours we know almost everything about the individual'. Most of the information gathered about contestants is from their social media accounts; so, '[i]t's like hanging your washing. You are putting pages of your life out on the line and allowing everybody to see it' (Virtue, 2015).

In the future Internet with automated surveillance via technology as the norm, this narrative—that if you put it out there, you need to be ready to bear the consequences—will only partially be accurate. Surveillance will be performed through 'surveillant assemblage' (Haggerty and Ericson, 2000) of many smart things. We will use them, first as early adopters, and then because they are cheap and/or life improvement devices. Soon, smart devices will be the only thing available on the market: there will be no other option but to buy a smart light bulb. Surveillance will prevail even if we decide to opt-out. Technology will sink into our unconscious, often unobserved and unchallenged. The purpose of technological and automated surveillance will be more than social sorting. Marginalised, over-policed, and silenced are likely to be disproportionately targeted by surveillance practices in the future, as it will be demonstrated in Chapter 3 in the context of AI. Nevertheless, the aim of surveillance will be surveillance *per se*, and everyone will be the target. 'Flying under the radar' might be the thing of the past, as AI-enabled technology such as autonomous mobile robots become your Amazon delivery couriers, and as your neighbour's Alexa suggests products and services based on what you eat at their house. This omnipresence of surveillant assemblage will be an important caveat when considering the role of emerging technologies in offending and crime control.

Actuarial automated justice: Predictive policing, pre-crime and automated administration of the law

Ubiquitous surveillance, pre-empting risk, and big data foster another crucial theoretical framework used in the book. Actuarial justice is the process of identifying, classifying, and managing suspect populations according to the level of risk they supposedly pose before they commit a crime or any other wrongdoing (Feeley and Simon, 1994). The backbone of actuarial justice is the identification of risk and anticipation of action: individuals and groups are thus observed and analysed as risk objects. Once mathematical calculations and algorithms identify risk, agencies deploy a range of strategies that manage risk and 'prevent' future crimes by incapacitating prospective offenders. All the elements of the criminal justice system follow this process: police, criminal courts, and probation agencies, as criminal justice organisations in the Global North and the Global South employ some form of 'algorithmic governance' (Danaher et al., 2017).

Predictive policing (or 'crime forecasting') is the flagship of algorithmic governance and the catchphrases of police practitioners (Wilson, 2018). It gained traction, particularly in the major cities in the United States. As the Chief of the Los Angeles Police Department stated in 2009,

> [v]ery soon we will be moving to a Predictive Policing model where, by studying real time crime patterns, we can anticipate where a crime is likely to occur.
>
> *(cited in Ferguson, 2012: 261)*

Today, the prediction of crime is 'the new watchword for innovative policing' (Ferguson, 2017: 1112). Predictive policing has generated quite an attention in the media and public discourse, so much so that the *TIME* magazine named it one of the 50 best inventions in 2011 (Grossman et al., 2011). The idea behind this 'smart' crime forecasting is that by using big data, both crime and not crime-related, we can identify not only probable future crimes and where they are likely to occur, but also prospective offenders and victims (Perry et al., 2013; Wilson, 2018). Identifying future risks via 'evidence-based' analytics is widely accepted as being more credible, scientific, and impartial than human-based analogue discretionary practices of relevant professionals (Hannah-Moffat, 2018). As such, policing that rests on 'traditional' methods of crime prevention are increasingly replaced with technocratic crime forecasting.

Ferguson (2017) identified three stages in the evolution of predictive policing practices in the US: Predictive Policing 1.0 focused on property crimes; 2.0 aimed to predict place-based violent crimes; and 3.0 concentrated on identifying future offenders. All systems involve computer models, algorithms that use big data to predict areas of future crime locations and/or perpetrators, and in theory, should assist police in distributing resources more effectively. As such, predictive policing is an extension of intelligence-led policing, but with a twist: in predictive policing, we do not identify past crime patterns, but the next crime location/offender based on the pattern (Ferguson, 2012). Identifying probable future offending underpins the idea that law enforcement can and should act before crime happens, with the help of technology. Welcome to the era of pre-crime, where agencies of social control aim to disrupt, incapacitate, restrict, and ultimately punish future crime threats

(McCulloch and Wilson, 2015). Introduced in Phillip K. Dick's short sci-fi story *Minority Report* and revived in the Hollywood blockbuster starring Tom Cruise, criminology focused on the concept of pre-crime since the early 2000s. Anticipatory logic of crimes that *have not* happened (and *may never* happen) and acting on them as they *did* happen, underpin pre-crime strategies. Post-crime approach, on the other hand, triggers the intervention with the commission of a crime, while risk-based crime prevention focuses on creating conditions in which a commission of a future criminal event is minimised. Pre-crime's attention is, as McCulloch and Wilson (2015) point out, on uncertain incalculable threats. As such, pre-crime strategies focus on many possible future scenarios that might never eventuate and penalise people for such 'behaviour'. After 9/11, Western democracies deployed a range of pre-crime based anti-terrorist interventions (McCulloch and Wilson, 2015; Wilson, 2018). It is the times of uncertainty in which pre-crime narratives thrive.

Data, it is often claimed, do not lie. As such, many practitioners and commentators hailed the system based on 'crunching' a large amount of data as a bias-free, objective method that can revolutionise policing in the future (Ferguson, 2017; Thomson, 2018). Yet, as Cathy O'Neill (2016: 3) skilfully argues,

> [t]he math-powered applications powering the data economy were based on choices made by fallible human beings. Some of these choices were no doubt made with the best intentions. Nevertheless, many of these models encoded human prejudice, misunderstanding, and bias into software systems that increasingly managed our lives. ... Their verdicts, even when wrong or harmful, were beyond dispute or appeal. And they tended to punish the poor and oppressed in our society, while making the rich richer.

As will be discussed in the following chapters, the limitations of big data and algorithms in crime control are significant. There are many critical deficiencies that we have to keep in mind when debating actuarial automated policing and justice: lack of transparency (we do not know where the data comes from and what is included), accuracy and ability to collect 'all' data about crime, error and potential bias ('garbage in–garbage out' argument concerning what crimes make it to crime statistics, for example), and unforeseeable social changes that impact on crime and offending come to mind. As Kitchin (2014), Chan and Bennett Moses (2016), and Broad (2018) note, even in the era of big data systems, data is simply a sample—it cannot capture all inputs. As such, big data occasionally has the effect of making-up data (Beer, 2016) and decisions based on it are likely flawed. Digital frontier technologies bring new challenges when it comes to predictive policing and algorithmic governance, especially given the development of AI. We are beholding a new development that aims to create 'master algorithms' able to process, learn, and adapt to decision-making that will not require (or tolerate) human input or control (Danaher et al., 2017). Devices and machines will be critical tools in actuarial justice-based pre-crime approach, in which the aim is to identify future offending and offenders via DFTs and disrupt them without human interference. Soon, algorithms are likely to be arresting, prosecuting, and sentencing people for future crimes they have not yet and may never commit. Critically, the system might be unfair, as algorithms do not have fairness and equality embedded in them.

The notion of 'objectivity' of data and algorithms underpin automated justice performed by criminal courts. Decisions on sentencing, parole, and bail delivered by humans, based on their expertise and experience, are now increasingly delegated to code. Such decisions are difficult to challenge because of the lack of transparency associated with big data and algorithms, and our lack of understanding of the process itself. Once humans are removed from this process, which is a possibility, protection of human rights and civil liberties will entirely be dependent on smart things. Yet, every algorithmic-based decision-making process has at the minimum two concerns identified above: efficiency and fairness (Danaher et al., 2017; see also Broad, 2018). Issues such as difficulties in predicting human behaviour, inaccuracy and flaws in big data, lack of transparency, arbitrariness, and lack of comprehension that things could exhibit in decision-making are harmful when an application for credit card gets wrongly rejected. They are profound if one gets arrested, prosecuted, convicted, or imprisoned because of an automated injustice.

Using more theories is always a good thing, right?

In addition to the above broader social and criminological theories, a range of specialised theoretical concepts will be used to unpack the complexities of DFTs. In Chapter 4, for example, I use the concept of the technological unconscious (Thrift, 2004; Beer, 2009; Wood, 2016) to explain the development and advancements of the IoT. The concept of the human–data assemblage (see Lupton, 2014) will be used to explore the expansion and impact of human to non-human and non-human to non-human relationships in AI and the IoT networks. In Chapter 3, when debating AI, Peter Asaro's concept of Model of Care (as opposed to Model of Threat) approach will be adopted in developing and applying AI. These and other theoretical models will add much-needed nuance in dissecting and forecasting the social in the future Internet.

Conclusion

Providing and applying theoretical insight to explain the developments in the future Internet will undoubtedly be a stretch. After all, the future of emerging digital technologies is anything but certain, as we do not know which technologies are going to make it, and what turn their expansion might take. Besides, as Bijker and Law (1992: 3) suggest,

> [t]echnologies always embody compromise. Politics, economics, theories of the strength of materials, notions about what is beautiful or worthwhile, professional preferences, prejudices and skills, design tools, available raw materials, theories about the behavior of the natural environment – all of these are thrown into the melting pot whenever an artefact is designed or built.

We also do not know what the impact of technological advancement on humans might be. Will we be obedient to the above processes as predicted? Will humans, 'in pursuit of health, happiness, and power … gradually change first one of their features and then another, and another, until they will no longer be human' (Harari, 2016: 49)? This book is an ambitious project, and as such, requires an ambitious theoretical reach. One overarching framework cannot explain similar yet diverse technologies such as the IoT and mobile robots, nor the framework(s) within one discipline or group of sciences. Such reach requires diving deep into a range of disciplines of STS, IT, and social sciences and criminology.

Undoubtedly, theorising DFTs is a challenging task. In the following chapters, I hope to commence the process by applying theoretical frameworks identified above that, in my opinion, are appropriate in this early phase of forecasting, exploring, and analysing a new world we are likely to live in very soon. As readers, you are invited to identify additional pathways, theories, and approaches that could be beneficial for the analysis of themes and processes covered in the book. To include your views and suggestions, a website for a collaborative scenario writing process accompanied the release of this book (www.crimetechbook.com). Professionals, students, laypersons, and experts from a range of disciplines are invited to engage in the debate and assist in designing future explorations of technology's impact on crime, offending, victimisation, and instruments of social control. This site will serve to exchange information, views, and insights, invite participants, propose, and engage in scenario development and analysis, collaborate and plan future research, develop action plans, and recommend policy-relevant and other future activities. Our present journey, however, commences with an overview of advancements and impact of artificial intelligence on crime and offending.

Notes

1 Such as naming and shaming as 'covidiots' citizens that failed or rejected to download the COVID-19 tracking application or adhere to public health measures that were designed and deployed to end lockdown – see Iqbal and Townsend (2020).
2 This is an argument/motto used in the debate for the expansion of CCTV surveillance in the UK – see Taylor (2010).
3 There is a scholarship in surveillance studies that looks at the extension of the panopticon vis-à-vis new technologies. I provide a very brief overview of the potential application of this concept in Chapter 4
4 While Bruno Latour often argued that ANT should not be applied as other social theories, this is precisely what I aim to do in this book – a bit of academic disobedience never goes astray. While I do risk to misapply the theory to the future Internet, I am happy to take that risk.
5 Even though the name of the theory uses this very term – see Lezaun (2017).

References

Andrejevic, M., 2012. Ubiquitous surveillance. In: Ball, K., Haggerty, K., Lyon, D. (Eds.), The Routledge Handbook of Surveillance Studies. Routledge, Abingdon Oxon, pp. 91–98.

Aradau, C., Blanke, T., 2017. Politics of prediction: Security and the time/space of governmentality in the age of big data. Eur. J. Soc. Theory 20 (3), 373–391.

Bauman, Z., 2000. Liquid Modernity. Polity, Cambridge.

Bauman, Z., Lyon, D., 2013. Liquid Surveillance. Polity, Cambridge.

Bean, R., CIO Network, 2020. Big Data In The Time Of Coronavirus (COVID-19). Forbes, 30 March.

Beck, U., Willms, J., 2004. Conversations with Ulrich Beck. Polity, Oxford.

Beer, D., 2009. Power through the algorithm? Participatory web cultures and the technological unconscious. N. Media Soc. 11 (6), 985–1002.

Beer, D., 2016. How should we do the history of Big Data? Big Data Soc. 3 (1), 2053951716646135.

Bennett Moses, L., Chan, J., 2014. Using Big Data for legal and law enforcement decisions: testing law enforcement decisions: testing the new tools. UNSW Law J. 37 (2), 643–678.

Bigo, D., 2002. Security and immigration: toward a critque of the governmentality of unease. Altern. Global Local Polit. 27 (1), 63–92.

Bigo, D., 2016. Rethinking security at the crossroad of international relations and criminology. Br. J. Criminol. 56 (6), 1068–1086.

Bijker, W., Law, J., 1992. General introduction, Shaping Technology/Building Society: Studies in Sociotechnical Change. MIT Press, Cambridge, pp. 1–14.

Blok, A., Jensen, T.E., 2011. Bruno Latour: Hybrid Thoughts in a Hybrid World. Routledge, London, United Kingdom.

Bostrom, N., Cirkovic, M., 2011. Global Catastrophic Risks. OUP Oxford, Oxford and New York.

boyd, d., Crawford, K., 2012. Critical questions for Big Data. Inf. Commun. Soc. 15 (5), 662–679.

Broad, E., 2018. Made by Humans: The AI Condition. Melbourne University Publishing, Melbourne.

Cale, J., Leclerc, B., Gil, F., 2020. Big data in criminology and criminal justice through the lens of the business literature. In: Leclerc, B., Cale, J. (Eds.), Big Data. Routledge, Abingdon and New York.

Callon, M., 1986. Some elements of a sociology of translation: domestication of the scallops and the fishermen of St. Brieuc Bay. Power Action Belief New Sociol. Knowl. 32, 196–223.

Chan, J., Bennett Moses, L., 2016. Is Big Data challenging criminology? Theor. Criminol. 20 (1), 21–39.

Danaher, J., Hogan, M.J., Noone, C., et al., 2017. Algorithmic governance: developing a research agenda through the power of collective intelligence. Big Data Soc. 4 (2), 2053951717726554.

Feeley, M., Simon, J., 1994. Actuarial justice: the emerging new criminal law. In: Nelken, D. (Ed.), The Futures of Criminology. Sage, London, pp. 173–201.

Ferguson, A.G., 2012. Predictive policing and the future of reasonable suspicion. Emory Law J. 62, 259–325.

Ferguson, A.G., 2017. Policing predictive policing. Wash. Univ. Law Rev. 94 (5), 1109–1189.

Finn, R.L., Wright, D., 2012. Unmanned aircraft systems: surveillance, ethics and privacy in civil applications. Comput. Law Secur. Rev. 28 (2), 184–194.

Goodman, M., 2016. Future Crimes: Inside the Digital Underground and the Battle for Our Connected World. Anchor Books, New York.

Grossman, L., Thompson, M., Kluger, J., et al. 2011. The 50 Best Inventions. TIME, 28 November.

Haggerty, K., Ericson, R., 2000. The surveillant assemblage. Br. J. Sociol. 51 (4), 605–622.

Hannah-Moffat, K., 2018. Algorithmic risk governance: Big data analytics, race and information activism in criminal justice debates. Theor. Criminol. 23 (4), 453–470.

Harari, Y.N., 2016. Homo Deus: A Brief History of Tomorrow. Random House, London.

Gray, C.H., et al., 1995. The cyborg handbook. Routledge, United Kingdom.

Haraway, D.J., Wolfe, C., 2016. Manifestly Haraway. University of Minnesota Press, Minneapolis, United States.

Hayward, K.J., Maas, M.M., 2020. Artificial intelligence and crime: A primer for criminologists. Crime Media Cult. doi:10.1177/1741659020917434.

HIMSS Media, 2020. Roundup: Tech's role in tracking, testing, treating COVID-19. Available from: https://www.mobihealthnews.com/news/roundup-techs-role-tracking-testing-treating-covid-19 (accessed 24.03.2020).

Huysmans, J., 2006. The Politics of Insecurity: Fear, Migration and Asylum in the EU. Routledge, London and New York.

Iqbal, N., Townsend, M., 2020. Duty or score-settling? Rights and wrongs of corona-shaming. The Guardian, 18 April.

Kitchin, R., 2014. The Data Revolution: Big Data, Open Data, Data Infrastructures and Their Consequences. SAGE Publications, Los Angeles, London, New Delhi, Singapore, Washington D.C.

Latour, B., 1996. On actor-network theory: a few clarifications. Soziale Welt 47, 369–381.

Latour, B., 1999. Pandora's Hope: Essays on the Reality of Science Studies. Harvard University Press, Cambridge.

Latour, B., 2005. Reassembling the Social: An Introduction to Actor-Network-Theory. OUP Oxford, Oxford.

Leman-Langlois, S., 2008. Technocrime: Technology, Crime and Social Control. Willan Publishing, Cullompton, United Kingdom.

Lezaun, J., 2017. Actor-network theory. In: Benzecry, C., Krause, M., Reed, I.A. (Eds.), Social Theory Now. University of Chicago Press, Chicago, pp. 305–337.

Lupton, D., 2014. Digital Sociology. Routledge, London, United Kingdom.

Lupton, D., 2016. Digital companion species and eating data: Implications for theorising digital data–human assemblages. Big Data Soc. 3 (1), 1–5.

Lupton, D., 2018. How do data come to matter? Living and becoming with personal data. Big Data Soc. 5 (2), 2053951718786314.

Lyon, D., 2007. Surveillance Studies. Polity, Cambridge.

Lyon, D., 2015. Surveillance after Snowden. Polity Press, Oxford, United Kingdom.

Marx, G., 2012. 'Your Papers please': personal and professional encounters with surveillance. In: Ball, K., Haggerty, K., Lyon, D. (Eds.), Routledge Handbook of Surveillance Studies. Routledge, London and New York, pp. XX–XXX.

Matthewman, S., 2011. Technology and Social Theory. Palgrave Macmillan, Basingstoke.

McCulloch, J., Wilson, D., 2015. Pre-Crime: Pre-Emption, Precaution and the Future. Routledge, London, United Kingdom.

McGuire, M., 2012. Technology, Crime and Justice: The Question Concerning Technomia. Routledge, London and New York.

Michael, M., 2016. Actor-Network Theory: Trials, Trails and Translations. Sage, London, Thousand Oaks, New Delhi, Singapore.

Milivojevic, S., 2019. Border Policing and Security Technologies. Routledge, London and New York.

O'Neill, C., 2016. Weapons of Math Destruction: How Big Data Increases Inequality and Threatens Democracy. Penguin Books, United Kingdom.

O'Neill, C., 2017. The era of blind faith in big data must end. TED2017 (ed). TED2017. Available from: https://www.ted.com/talks/cathy_o_neil_the_era_of_blind_faith_in_big_data_must_end?language=en (accessed 1 September 2020).

Perry, W., McInnis, B., Price, C., et al., 2013. Predictive Policing The Role of Crime Forecasting in Law Enforcement Operations. RAND Corporation, United States.

Porter J. 2020. The latest USB-C chargers are apparently more powerful than Apollo 11's computer. Available from: https://www.theverge.com/tldr/2020/2/11/21133119/usb-c-anker-charger-apollo-11-moon-landing-guidance-computer-more-powerful (accessed 1.09.2020).

Poster, M., 1990. The Mode of Information: Poststructuralism and Social Context. Polity, Cambridge.

Powell, A., Stratton, G., Cameron, R., 2018. Digital Criminology: Crime and Justice in Digital Society. Routledge, Milton, United Kingdom.

Qiang, X., 2019. The road to digital unfreedom: President Xi's surveillance state. J. Democracy 30 (1), 53–67.

Taylor, E., 2010. Evaluating CCTV: Why the findings are inconsistent, inconclusive and ultimately irrelevant. Crime. Prev. Commun. Saf. 12 (4), 209–232.

Thomson S., 2018. 'Predictive policing': law enforcement revolution or just new spin on old biases? Depends who you ask. Available from: https://www.cbc.ca/news/world/crime-los-angeles-predictive-policing-algorithms-1.4826030 (accessed 3.04.2020).

Thrift, N., 2004. Remembering the Technological Unconscious by Foregrounding Knowledges of Position. Environ. Plan. D: Soc. Space 22 (1), 175–190.

Virtue, G., 2015. Hunted: could you go on the run in our post-Snowden surveillance state? The Guardian, 29 August.

Wæver, O., 1995. Securitization and desecuritization. In: Lipschutz, R.D. (Ed.), On Security. Columbia University Press, New York Chichester, pp. 46–86.

Walker, S., 2020. Authoritarian leaders may use Covid-19 crisis to tighten their grip. The Guardian, 31 March.

Wall, D., 2018. How big data feeds big crime. Global His. J. Contemp. World Aff. (January 2018), 29–34.

Wilson, D., 2018. Algorithmic patrol: The future of predictive policing. In: Završnik, A. (Ed.), Big Data, Crime and Social Control. Routledge, London and New York.

Wood, M.A., 2016. Antisocial media and algorithmic deviancy amplification: analysing the id of Facebook's technological unconscious. Theor. Criminol. 21 (2), 168–185.

Završnik, A., 2018. Big data: What is it and why does it matter for crime and social control? In: Završnik, A. (Ed.), Big Data, Crime and Social Control. Routledge, London and New York.

Zedner, L., 2009. Security. Routledge, London, United Kingdom.

Zedner, L., 2010. Security, the state, and the citizen: the changing architecture of crime control. N. Crim. Law Rev. Int. Interdiscip. J. 13 (2), 379–403.

3

ARTIFICIAL INTELLIGENCE AND MACHINE LEARNING

The backbone of the human-thing alliance

Introduction

At its heart, artificial intelligence is computer programming that learns and adapts (Pichai, 2018). In the focus of the scientific community since the mid-1940s, the earliest work generally recognised as AI was in the field of computational neuroscience, done by Warren McCulloch and Walter Pitts in 1943 (Russel and Norvig, 2016). Computer scientist John McCarthy coined the term in 1956, defining AI as 'the science and engineering of making intelligent machines' (Goodman, 2016: 469). More recently, physicist Max Tegmark (2017) defined AI as a non-biological intelligence, while intelligence is the ability to accomplish complex goals. Russel and Norvig (2016) suggest that AI is the process of designing and building intelligent agents that receive precepts from the environment and, by taking actions, change the environment. The commercial use of artificial intelligence commenced in the late 1970s and early 1980s; since then, AI and its subset machine learning have advanced to the point that 'systems are now capable of learning how to accomplish a task without having been provided with explicit steps for doing so' (United Nations, 2018: 33). In the era of big data, over 10,000 scientists work on different aspects of creating intelligent things. Yet, only about 100 people in the world work on addressing limitations in our under-standing of AI and its abilities, while only about ten have formal training needed for such work (Yampolskiy, 2019). Such disproportionality is puzzling given the recent surge of scientists, futurists, business leaders, philosophers, and social commentators concerned about the emergence of 'strong' AI (Artificial general intelligence - AGI) as an ability of things or software to accomplish any goal at least as well as humans (Tegmark, 2017).

Artificial intelligence is one of the topics that everyone has an opinion on, be it good or bad. Regardless of expertise on the matter or awareness of AI around us, we are:

- *Luddites* who consider AI in general and AGI, in particular, a bad thing and oppose its development;
- *Techno-sceptics* who argue AGI is unlikely to happen anytime soon;
- Members of the *Beneficial AI* movement, uncertain about whether AGI is going to be good or bad but willing to give it a go, with safety research and other safeguards in place to prevent a bad outcome; or
- *Digital utopians* who trust that AGI is ultimately going to benefit humankind and enable space exploration (Tegmark, 2017).

The debate is sharp and often uncompromising. Six years ago, one of the world's leading scientists, Professor Stephen Hawking, suggested that AI 'could spell the end of the human race' (Cellan-Jones, 2014; Hawking et al., 2014). 'Whereas the short-term impact of AI depends on who controls it', he argued, 'the long-term impact depends on whether it can be controlled at all' (Stephen Hawking, cited in Hawking et al., 2014). Leading thinkers and inventors such as Nick Bostrom, Elon Musk, Bill Gates, Steve Wozniak, Max Tegmark, and others routinely address the 'control problem' of AI. Futurist and author Nikola Danaylov (2016: Section 10 Reasons to Fear Technological Singularity, subsection 1) suggests that extinction of human race is 'by far the most feared as well as the most commonly predicted consequence' of AI expansion. On the other hand, Larry Page from Google leads digital utopians, suggesting that AGI is the next natural and desirable step in our cosmic evolution (Tegmark, 2017).

There are many common myths and misconceptions about AI (see Tegmark, 2017; Chase, 2018). One is that AI will develop consciousness, turn 'evil' and wipe us out from the face of the planet via objects, devices, and machines powered by smart algorithms (Harari, 2018: 68–70; see also Goodman, 2016; Schneider, 2019). As Yampolskiy would have it, although the end of civilisation might happen at some point, this will not be because AI gains self-awareness and destroys humanity. If such attrocity happens, it will be for human actions in relation to AI[1]. Indeed, AI might turn competent at some point, and its goals might misalign with ours; this is the real danger we might face in the future (Tegmark, 2017; Bostrom, 2017; Future of Life Institute, 2020). Although I will touch on the issue of 'strong' AI in this volume, given that this is primarily a philosophical and computer science question and not essential to the aims of this book, it is best to leave it for philosophers, AI researchers, and tech leaders.

The focus of this chapter is the link between AI, crime and institutions of social control. Artificial intelligence, for example, has long been singled out as a critical technology to support police operations (Brahan et al., 1998). As Harari (2018: 29) implies, drawing on a famous example of AI-human cooperation in chess that outperformed both humans and computers, machine learning systems and AI might help us 'groom' the best police detectives in history. The question, however, is whether we over-estimate the developments and future trajectory of technology, often influenced by science fiction and the entertainment industry? What precarious developments should we be wary of? How far shall we go in our foresight approach? After offering an overview of the origins, types, and advances of AI, this chapter explores the three areas of inquiry:

- AI, the law, and offending;
- Bias and error in AI applications; and
- AI and the criminal justice system.

The final section is dedicated to theorising AI, followed by the conclusion with some key pointers for future research in this exciting yet somewhat daunting area of technological progress.

The origins, types, and developments of AI

It was a conference held in 1955 at Dartmouth College in the US that inaugurated the term 'artificial intelligence'. The conference gathered 20 scientists from various disciplines interested in the field of 'thinking machines' and kindled a new area of scientific research, with many participants becoming leaders in the field[2]. Like many other technological discoveries, there is no universally accepted definition of AI. Russel and Norvig (2016: 2) suggest that there are four dimensions within which a range of AI definitions develop:

- Thinking humanly;
- Acting humanly (human-centred approaches);

- Thinking rationally; and
- Acting rationally (rationalist approaches).

Human-centred approaches link AI to the functioning of humans. For example, acting humanly approach would consider that a system is AI if a human interrogator cannot tell whether the written response to their questions come from a person or a device/machine (this is the premise of the celebrated Turing test, proposed by Alan Turing in 1950). AI, thus, would be 'creating computer programs or machines capable of behavior we would regard as intelligent if exhibited by humans' (Kaplan, 2016: 1). Rationalist approaches move away from human-thing comparison. They look at the things that would 'solve any solvable problems described in logical notation', or whether the systems are rational agents that would act to achieve the best outcome in a given situation (Russel and Norvig, 2016: 4).

A subset of AI is machine learning comprised of systems able to solve the problem by picking their own parameters from a range of different parameters available, and with limited or no input from the outside world. Machine learning systems, thus, learn and improve through their own experience and input (Tegmark, 2017). Machine learning can be supervised, reinforced, or unsupervised. Ellen Broad (2018) offers a handy metaphor to understand different types of machine learning: a cooking recipe. In supervised learning, a computer is given pre-labelled data (some ingredients, a picture of how the meal looks like and how it should taste) and is required to identify rules and patterns to produce the desired outcome. Unsupervised learning is when devices or machines have no pointers to identify the inputs (recipe, ingredients), outputs (a meal), and rules linking the two (for supervised and unsupervised learning see also Kitchin, 2014). Reinforced learning is the system that feeds from the environment, discovering by trial and error how to 'win' or maximise the score metrics (Chase, 2018; Hayward and Maas, 2020). Machine learning is one of the fastest evolving scientific fields. In April 2020, scientists at Google succeeded in creating a software that uses the Darwinian concept of evolution and can improve future generations of software with no human input other than the basic mathematical concepts (Gent, 2020). However, as witnessed in a recent example of machine-learning language generating system GPT-3, intelligent agents struggle to pass human-like text. When presented with a scenario of a lawyer with a dirty suit but clean bathers, GPT-3 suggested that a lawyer should wear a bathing suit in court (Marcus and Davis, 2020).

Intelligent behaviour is commonly required if we want to classify a system as AI. Intelligence incorporates five key attributes: communication (the higher the level of communication, the higher the intelligence), internal knowledge (knowledge about self), external knowledge (knowledge about the outside world), goal-driven behaviour or taking actions to achieve its goals, and creativity as the ability to take alternate actions if the initial one fails (see Hallevy, 2010: 175–176). Some types of artificial intelligence used today arguably tick all the above boxes (think, for example, Google Nest that integrates surveillance and protection of your property with temperature regulation, entertainment system control, and more). Notwithstanding the astute critique of the view of AI that seeks to separate the comparison to human intelligence (see Kaplan, 2016), the technology in popular culture seems to be conceptualised through its performance in the various human-thing contest. Many see IBM Deep Blue's victory over the chess champion Gary Kasparov in 1997 (after which Kasparov famously suggested that he felt 'a new kind of intelligence' sitting across from him; Russel and Norvig, 2016: 29) and IBM Watson's 2011 triumph in *Jeopardy!* as crown achievements of AI. Google Alpha Go also triumphed in the ancient game of Go in 2016 (see Kaplan, 2016; Tvede, 2020). The above are examples of narrow AI that performs a specific task; we can easily recognise it—from Siri to Amazon Echo. Narrow AI has the superior *computational ability*, but its *learning* is *limited*, mostly dependent on large datasets we feed them. Narrow AI also focuses on specific tasks. On the other hand, AGI or strong AI will be generalised intelligence that is likely to outcompete us in all cognitive tasks (see Tegmark, 2017). Some authors argue that AGI is only several decades away (Schneider, 2019) and predict it to be the biggest event in human history (Future of Life Institute, 2020). This occurrence will be the dawn of *technological singularity*—a point where AI surpasses human intelligence, with unpredictable consequences for our civilisation. As Kevin Kelly, co-founder of the WIRED magazine suggests, singularity can be described as a point at which 'all the change in the last million years will be superseded by the change in the next five minutes' (Jennings, 2019: 32). AGI has been driving the debate in academia and popular culture, adored or mocked as 'the rapture of the geeks' (Tegmark, 2017). Although fascinating, the singularity is not the focus of the book, and this is where we leave it but not before pointing out a range of literature if you wish to explore this topic further (Kurzweil, 2005; Danaylov, 2016; Bostrom, 2017; Tegmark, 2017; Walsh, 2017; Schneider, 2019). What might be of importance to criminologists and social scientists, however, is a sentiment put forward by Kelly (cited in Danaylov, 2016: Section Kevin Kelly, Subsection The Dangers of AI):

> One of the things that we don't fully appreciate is that AIs, as we make them more and more complex, we will be less and less able to understand how they arrived at a decision and we'll be trusting those decisions.

While the quest for 'explainable AI' that provides reasoning for its outputs continues (Phillips et al., 2020), the issue of AI's non-transparency remains of utmost importance for social scientists. Other challenges we might encounter if and when we get closer to developing strong AI will be highlighted in the book but not at length. An in-depth analysis is not warranted (yet), as experts disagree on the possibility of timing for strong AI emergence. What is indisputable, however, is the likely impact of existing and future 'narrow' AI systems on offending and criminal justice.

Scanning and scenario writing: Artificial intelligence, law, offending and crime control

The ultimate criminal? When smart things do the wrong thing

Machine learning algorithms play an essential role in the social fabric for decades. Facial recognition software, virtual personal assistants, product suggestions, car autopilots, search and movie recommendations are some prominent examples. There is an almost universal agreement among scholars and practitioners that legal systems are trailing behind when it comes to AI development. Within a broader 'crimes with AI, crimes against AI, and crimes by AI' framework (Hayward and Maas, 2020), the first question that needs unpacking is whether AI-powered devices and machines should be subject to criminal law. One might argue this question is more appropriate for science fiction than academia, or comparable to debates vis-à-vis medieval trials of dogs for criminal conduct (Hildebrandt, 2008). However, the matter is both complex and relevant. In the early 1980s, a robot in a Japanese motorcycle factory pushed a worker into an adjacent operating machine after identifying the human as a threat to its mission (Hallevy, 2010). While this was not the first case of a death caused by a smart machine and while such incidents are extremely rare (Tegmark, 2017), the case sparked a debate in academia about AI's potential in assisting/committing a crime (Hayward and Maas, 2020; King et al., 2020). From malware, phishing attacks, identity thefts, blackmail, frauds, market manipulations, and 'deep fakes' to assaults and homicide, AI systems' potential in enabling and carrying out criminal acts is undisputable. As I explore later in the book, AI can also be hacked/manipulated and turned to malicious use.

Recently, autonomous weapons with AI technology have been singled out as one of the great dangers for humankind (Slijper, 2019; this question will be explored in detail in Chapter 5). But when AI offends because of malfunctioning software or because its goals were misaligned with ours, who is responsible? The issue of criminal liability leads to the debate around AI ethics and whether technological artefacts—devices and machines—need to be considered ethical agents (for a comprehensive overview of this issue, see Verbeek, 2011). Currently, AI systems are not subject to criminal law and have no legal rights or duties. Smart things, it is commonly argued, do not have mind, consciousness, free will or intentionality and cannot be held responsible for their actions (Verbeek, 2011). The question I begin to unpack below is whether we need to re-think this approach given the advances in, and impact of technology, and whether we should consider smart objects as moral agents in themselves—entities that can perform actions, for good or evil. This issue, it seems, is particularly important given their increased autonomy within growing thing-to-thing and thing-to-human networks. Floridi and Sanders' (2004) influential theory of the moral agency of intelligent technologies and ANT constitute a broad framework for the upcoming analysis. They suggest that technological artefacts need to have interactivity, autonomy, and adaptability to become moral agents. Artificial intelligence and machine learning systems tick all the above boxes. They are actants, as humans are no longer sole actors in the social setting. Non-humans (such as DFTs) and their users/consumers create hybrids that act as mediators, as defined inputs do not translate into defined outputs; *ergo,* crime occurs, despite carefully crafted code by software developers and a correct usage by the consumers. As such, it is time to think about criminal liability that is not (or not exclusively) linked to their human companions.

In common law, criminal liability has two key elements: *actus reus*—a factual, external element, criminal conduct, and *mens rea*—an internal, mental element, knowledge, or general intent towards *actus reus*. The guiding principle is *actus reus non facit reum nisi mens sit rea* ('the act does not make one guilty unless the mind is also guilty'). *Mens rea* can be the knowledge about *actus reus*, or negligence (about something a reasonable person should know). If one of these elements is missing, no criminal liability can be established for many offences in common law systems. *Actus reus* is contentious when it comes to AI agents, but it is plausible. *Mens rea*, however, is mostly considered in conjunction with a human who possesses *mens rea*, while AI commits *actus reus* (King et al., 2020). It is because of *mens rea* that some authors suggest we should seek to establish criminal liability elsewhere, not with the 'thinking machines' themselves. For example, Goodman (2016) suggests we need to investigate computer coders, as they should be responsible if AI systems break the law. The code, he argues, is the brain of smart things but is ultimately the product of human design. Hallevy (2010), on the other hand, outlines three models of AI criminal liability: the perpetration-via-another, the natural-probable-consequence, and the direct liability model. The first two models are dependency models, linked to humans, in which AI is not an independent entity. In the perpetrator-via-another, AI systems have capabilities that might be comparable to the capabilities of a child, or a person who is mentally incapacitated. This is the liability system we have today for child soldiers, who also do not have *mens rea* (Perry and Roda, 2016). As such, legally, they are innocent agents, and criminal liability is established elsewhere. In the case of a child who commits a crime as instructed by the parent or army commanders, they are the ones who will be held liable. If AI commits a crime, it will be software developers or end-users, as *mens rea* is established in a person who developed or operated the system. This model is human-centric and is not suitable in cases where AI was not designed to commit a specific offence or when a crime is committed based on code that AI develops by itself. The natural-probable-consequence liability model does not look for *mens rea* but at coders or users' ability to foresee the potential commission of offences as a natural and probable consequence of AI systems' actions.

In the direct liability model, AI systems are the ones legally sanctioned. Hallevy (2010: 187) argues that attributing *actus reus* to AI devices or machines is relatively easy, but the internal element is 'the real legal challenge in most cases'. To establish knowledge, intent, or negligence of AI systems is complicated but conceivable, and AI could be criminally liable regardless of liability of humans. As Kaplan (2016: 106) suggests, '[t]here is no reason you can't write a program that knows what it is doing, knows it is illegal (and presumably therefore unethical), and can make a choice as to what actions to take'. This concern is called *emergence*, and it refers to the process of AI agents acting beyond the ways originally intended by developers, or, to use ANT terminology—become actants/mediators. Computer coders can and often do 'encourage' specific scenarios undertaken by the AI; nevertheless, AI systems can and do take a particular pathway autonomously, without human interference (see King et al., 2020). They undoubtedly have interactivity, autonomy, and adaptability, and use these skills for either morally good or evil. Thus, they are within 'aresponsible' or 'mind-less' morality, within which intention or guilty mind is not necessary for accountability (Floridi and Sanders, 2004). If devices and machines learn independently from humans and develop/alter code, is it therefore prudent to look at them vis-à-vis criminal liability? After we address this question, the next quest to ponder is an appropriate punishment for AI (Hildebrandt, 2008; for some ideas, see Hallevy, 2010) and what rights, if any, should extend to AI systems (Gunkel, 2020). My intention here is not to dig deep into the legal philosophy and theory; I am simply flagging concerns legal scholars and criminologists already face. These questions will be of utmost importance given the development of emerging digital technologies in the smart cities of the future.

One of the objectives for AI development at Google is that the technology should be socially beneficial and ought to avoid creating or reinforcing unfair bias (Pichai, 2018). Therefore, as its leading developers acknowledge, AI systems could and indeed often do reproduce and bolster unfair biases and discrimination (Yampolskiy, 2019; Broad, 2018). One of the most notorious examples is Tay, an ill-fated Microsoft chatbot. Developed to mimic the language patterns of young Americans and programmed to learn from interactions with punters on Twitter, Tay turned into an aggressive racist, Nazi fan and a bigot within hours of being operational. Microsoft shut down the experiment 16 hours after the launch (Chase, 2018; Bunz and Meikle, 2018).

AI's 'neutrality' has long been debated in popular culture and academia. Harari (2018: 60) suggest that if we program the software so that it ignores race, gender, and class, 'computer will indeed ignore these factors because computers don't have a subconscious'. Goodman (2016), Broad (2018) and O'Neill (2016), however, claim that human bias saturates existing algorithms. As Cathy O'Neill famously declared, 'algorithms are opinions embedded in code' (O'Neill, 2017: 1:40). They, she continues, need two key things to be built: past data and the definition of success. Sexism, racism, xenophobia, and other forms of discrimination do not exist in a bubble and are embedded in past data. Removing embedded bias that exists in large annotated datasets AI systems use for training is difficult. Virginia Eubanks in *Automating Inequality* powerfully demonstrates how algorithms reinforce (if not further produce) inequality in three critical areas of public services in the United States: homelessness, welfare provision, and child protection services (Eubanks, 2017). It is also hard to prevent programmers and engineers from inserting their own subconscious biases into code. Indeed, as the next segment indicates, the notion that AI can further inequalities has had significant consequences when it comes to crime control in the Global North.

As suggested in Chapter 2, actuarial justice has achieved its renaissance in the twenty-first century. To predict offending and recidivism, government agencies rely on AI and big data, especially in the United States and to a lesser extent, the United Kingdom and continental Europe (see Gerritsen, 2020). Applying algorithms and machine learning systems to large datasets to forecast where crimes are likely to occur and who might commit them has been at the forefront of what some commentators have called 'digital policing revolution' (EMPAC, 2017). The modelling usually ties future offending to places (Predictive Policing 1.0 and 2.0) and people (Predictive Policing 3.0) based on age, criminal record and history, employment, and their social affiliations. Thus, crime and environmental data assist in predicting where and when police officers should patrol the streets to deter or detect crime (Shapiro, 2017). But just what data do they use and what is the definition of success?

One of the well-known examples of machine learning 'crime risk forecasting' systems was *HunchLab*[3]. The web-based system analysed records of historical crime data in certain areas as well as current crime reports, emergency calls made by the public, geographical features (such as train stations, pubs, and bridges), environmental factors (lighting), social data (major events and gatherings), time of the year, day of the week, weather reports and the like (Chammah and Hansen, 2016; Joh, 2017b; Cheetam, 2019). Based on a vast amount of data—some of which embeds existing bias in crime reporting and processing—*HunchLab* signalled areas where potential crime might happen. Importantly, while *HunchLab* did use non-crime related data, it did not use data about people, nor was it focused on predicting people's actions. The developers also intentionally excluded data about prior arrests and convictions, social media, and other personal data, and drew on multiple, independent sources (not just law enforcement data) in an attempt to avoid bias (Cheetam, 2019). Founders of *HunchLab* sold the business in 2018 after they realised the product might lead to over-policing of certain social groups, civil rights violations, and abuse of power (although they cited business reasons as the key driver for sale; see Cheetam, 2019)[4].

Many contemporary predictive policing and offending interventions have been criticised as racist (Shapiro, 2017; Joh, 2017a; Angwin et al., 2016; Broad, 2018; Završnik, 2018; Gerritsen, 2020) or otherwise discriminatory (Ferguson, 2012). The literature and research suggest that predictive policing strategies disproportionately target minority neighbourhoods (Chammah and Hansen, 2016; Shapiro, 2017). Studies have found that black people were 77% more likely to be predicted to perpetrate a future violent crime, and 45% more likely to be predicted to commit any crime than non-black populations. At the same time, AI systems fail to predict crime: only 20% of people the system predicted to commit a violent crime did so (Cush, 2016; Angwin et al., 2016). Crime forecasting strategies underpinned by racially biased policing data integrate these biases into the analyses, and police who find criminally suspicious behaviour based on these predictions reinforce biases. If patrol cars sent to prevent burglary find a couple of youth swinging from a bottle and acting suspiciously, they will arrest them, creating 'pernicious feedback loop' (O'Neill, 2016): they create data to justify more policing.

In the era of the exponential growth of computing abilities and Moore's Law[5] that predict that the processing power of computers doubles every two years (Chase, 2018), we will see the dramatic changes in predictive policing and automated justice that could have harmful consequences for many. With the development of AI, we might soon witness the emergence of Predictive Policing 4.0, based on machine-learning pre-emption. The logic here will not be to identify where future crimes might happen or even who is going to perpetrate them, but to use algorithms to forestall offending altogether. Strategies to prevent a likely event (however loosely defined) have been replaced by addressing uncertain and incalculable threats. With the development of DFTs, we are a step closer to 'substantive coercive state interventions targeted at non-imminent crimes' (McCulloch and Wilson, 2015: 5). Artificial intelligence systems, it is argued, could do this by removing humans from the process of decision-making. The pace of AI expansion and systems' learning abilities is so fast that, if we remain passive, we risk that tomorrow's technology might challenge us in a way we cannot foresee. Perhaps not to the extent of an end-of-life-on-Earth scenario, but in a way where key postulates of our legal and social order could irrevocably shift. This is not to suggest that technological singularity or strong AI will become a reality. However, we cannot ignore the pace of the development in AI and machine learning, and need to be prepared (as much as possible) for potential consequences this expansion might bring for years to come. Smart algorithms might become super-efficient enforcement agents that promptly detect and punish every violation of the law, with an intent to do so (we see rudiments of this approach in China's social credit policy, in which jaywalking or crossing on red light results in losing points and certain rights; see Kobie, 2019; Chase, 2018). They will be on 24/7 and will not ignore our (actual or future) violations. There will be no need for police, courts, judges, or appeal. As I explore later in the book, systems' decision will be final, irrevocable, and penalty will occur regardless of who the transgressors are and whether they are likely to commit the crime in the future. We are apt to believe in the fairness of such decisions, as we falsely trust the notion that things are impartial and have no bias. But, given that we are not quite there yet, what is the point in worrying about it? Even if we reach this stage at some point, many argue the above scenario might not be so bad after all. Uncertainty and threats are everywhere around us, and given that humans are deeply flawed and not capable of rising to the task, why not let the smart things do the job for us? I come to this pivotal point in the final segment of this chapter.

Other scenarios, however, are more plausible, at least in the immediate future. It is likely, for example, that AI-based predictive policing will incorporate data that *HunchLab* refused to embed in its system—data about people, including records and inputs collected and provided via fitness trackers or IoT devices—to predict future crimes and identify offenders. In the era of ever-growing big data and underpinned by continuous surveillance and monitoring of potential suspects, algorithms will be assessing and determining their (and our) likely behaviour, which might lead to further pre-crime interventions. In *the Minority Report*, the mutated humans called precogs previsualise future offences, prompting law enforcement to react before crimes occur. In the AI-based future, the focus will be on offenders, but not exclusively those who have previously offended or people affiliated with other lawbreakers and gangs. Algorithms will calculate the likelihood to offend, based on a range of big data about you, such as your habits, associations, and overall digital footprint. As pre-crime approach is largely speculative, the use of technology will make it appear evidence-based. In other words, the process will provide the illusion of scientific neutrality (McCulloch and Wilson, 2015). If AI is likely to reinforce the stereotypes already entrenched in our society, this new pre-crime approach will fundamentally change the way we engage with crime and offending, and not in a good way. Critically, this development is likely to be an ultimate *blackboxing* moment Bruno Latour (1999: 304) and others warned about a while ago. The more technology succeeds, the more obscure and opaque it will become; we will be aware of inputs and outputs but not the internal complexity of the artefacts and smart things.

AI detectives: Actuarial justice on steroids

Artificial intelligence has been pinpointed as a game-changer when it comes to solving crimes and apprehending offenders. Innovations such as *VALCRI* are an example of this narrative. *VALCRI* or Visual Analytics for Sense-Making in Criminal Intelligence Analysis is the AI-based system that scans and processes police records, pictures, interviews, and other data to identify patterns missed by human analysts and solve unresolved and historical crimes (Revell, 2017; Baraniuk, 2019). Processing a vast number of images, extracting information from it, and making conclusions and links is predicted to revolutionise detectives' work in the future. It could, as some commentators claim, entirely eliminate the need for human detectives (Revell, 2017). While systems such as *VALCRI* are expensive and are currently available mainly to law enforcement in the Global North, other AI-based technologies are becoming mainstream in crime control. A type of AI-based technology widely used by law enforcement is facial recognition software. This technology is particularly useful in identifying victims of child sexual abuse, in which the trauma of going through hundreds or thousands of pictures of abuse is replaced by devices and machines that swiftly identify, classify, and process victims and potential victims. Facial recognition has also been used to identify and 'rescue' victims of sex trafficking (Baraniuk, 2019). AI and machine learning systems also assist in identifying offenders when their identity is unknown (for example, when offender's face is obscured by a helmet, or there is a partial or blurry photo of a face). Discovering and preventing online fraud is another area where AI systems have been delivering impressive results. These initiatives are especially pervasive in the United States (Rigano, 2019), but can they be trusted? Can interested parties challenge the decisions made by AI systems in court? Some critics warn that this might not be possible, given the proprietary rights of the technology is with businesses that develop and sell it to government agencies (O'Neill, 2017; Baraniuk, 2019).

Nevertheless, in the smart cities of the future, the use of AI-based systems in crime control is likely to grow. As weak AI slowly transitions to more robust AI systems, humans will increasingly rely on code to do the 'legwork' in criminal investigations. Data these systems access will not be what we 'feed' them willingly, to train learning algorithms. AI systems will likely have access to our social media (or the future equivalent of Facebook, Twitter, or Instagram), mobile phones and computers, sensors embedded in the IoT, data about a crime scene or a potential suspect from government agencies and businesses, and more. Finally, criminal trials will increasingly rely on algorithms (Bennett Moses and Chan, 2014). The driver behind such development is a promise of eradicating racial, gendered, or other bias from courtrooms (see Tegmark, 2017). In fact, smart algorithms are already in use in pretrial, parole, and sentencing decisions especially in the United States. So-called 'recidivism models' are deployed in over 20 state jurisdictions, with code assisting judges in assessing danger posed by offenders (O'Neill, 2016). While race is not one of the factors considered in such systems, other issues correlated with race are, such as the criminal history of family members, prior associations with the police, and the like (Broad, 2018). Machine learning algorithms of the future might—after processing a vast amount of data from personal information, financial and travel history, affiliations, prior convictions, sentences, and the list goes on—make decisions on bail, parole applications, and sentencing without human input. This is the second *blackboxing* moment identified in this chapter. Without transparency and understanding of the process in which things decide to refuse or approve bail, and without an opportunity to question such decisions, we might face a devastating blow for basic human rights and civil liberties. Smart systems may, yet again, turn to be mediators, and the output of their actions may not be aligned with our goal of a fair, just, and transparent criminal justice system.

From pre-crime to Model Of Care: Theorising AI and crime

The development of AI is likely to result in a fundamental redesign of our legal system and criminal justice responses. Even if we abstain from the debate on the likelihood of AGI and consciousness of self-learning systems (and questions such as if a conscious machine serves us presumably without pay would this constitute a situation akin to slavery – see Tegmark, 2017; Schneider, 2019; Gunkel, 2020), dramatic changes might be just around the corner. This emerging digital technology will undoubtedly modify everyday life, to the extent that we struggle to envision right now. The hybrid AI-human systems we enjoy today and the ones we might have in the future are likely mediators that could lead to many (un)wanted crime-related consequences, some of which are outlined in this chapter. Importantly, our understanding of the technology—how it works, how it comes to certain decisions, or how to challenge it—is expected to decrease.

Surveillance will not be the only basis for the likely supremacy of the AI systems. The argument of 'life improvement' will continue to drive the exponential growth of this technology. The question is: what happens when the algorithms do not improve our lives? Should we 'punish' AI systems for offences they commit? Should machine learning systems be legal and moral agents, and as such, be held criminally liable when *actus reus* is present? What happens as technology develops, and we come closer to technological singularity? Do we need to start thinking outside of the box and reconsider the fundamental principles of criminal justice and criminal law now, before we have the problem at hand?

As suggested earlier, pre-crime represents one of the fundamental shifts in contemporary engagement with offending and crime control that aims to identify future threats, 'predict' crime, and strike before a crime occurs. This strategy is not underpinned by reducing opportunities or the means for offending, which is at the very core of crime prevention interventions. Crime prevention implies the curtailment of a future, likely event. Pre-crime is focused on many possible and projected futures that may or may not happen. It is imagining, designing, planning future crimes, or simply being pinpointed as the future perpetrator that triggers the intervention. The objective is to disrupt, incapacitate, punish those singled out as future offenders via a variety of technology and non-technology-based interventions. With advances in AI, it is easy to imagine that pre-crime might become commonplace where algorithms provide 'evidence' for uncertain incalculable threats. In the context where many threats are deemed as imminent, the argument that it would be for the best if smart things take the reins flourishes. While we do not always have faith in impartiality and objectivity of human decisions, we ought to trust devices and machines even less. This scepticism is necessary because such developments might lead to pre-crime interventions and because of the haphazard nature of current technological progress. Importantly, these processes challenge the notion of criminal liability, but in a vastly different way compared to the one discussed above. In cases of pre-crime-based criminal justice, there is no *actus reus* at all, all the while smart algorithms, on the surface so scientific and bullet-proof, rest on fragmentary and biased big data.

Therefore, it is essential to reconsider the philosophy that drives AI advances. Here, I draw on the works of Peter Asaro, one of the leading philosophers of science, technology, and media. Asaro (2019) suggests that in discussing AI, we need a new approach. Things around us are already 'bursting with morality'[6], and ethics is no longer only a human affair (Verbeek, 2011: 2). Hybrid systems of today can perform actions, for good and evil. Yet, the approach we see in AI development is mostly based on human ethics. The Model of Threat approach is widely used in developing contemporary machine learning and AI systems, including the ones used in crime control. The assumption that everything falls into two categories—threats and non-threats—underpins the above approach. This narrative applies to the majority of contemporary responses to crime and offending. AI systems, thus, are tasked to identify threats and develop strategies to eliminate or reduce crime-related threats. The idea is that through machine learning and large datasets, sophisticated AI will be more accurate, precise, and comprehensive in evaluating the risk of (re)offending of observed populations. Most of the systems used today and discussed in this chapter are examples of the Model of Threat AI systems.

A contrario, the Model of Care approach would see the development of AI actors based on values and goals that should benefit everyone in the system (human and non-human), those who use the system, and the society. This method is largely non-binary. It is based on the understanding that social relations and contexts are not linear; instead, they are incredibly complex, and more and better data do not necessarily translate into solutions for existing social and institutional problems. Nonetheless, better and bigger data might provide opportunities to find solutions for the problem at hand and improve existing policy frameworks. Rather than looking to identify and predict future violations of the law, including future offenders, Asaro argues that AI systems should help us understand why people offend and focus on crime prevention, rather than pre-crime. By identifying young people at the risk of offending and providing them with jobs, for example, researchers using not-so-state-of-the-art technology in the city of Chicago managed to reduce violence-related arrests among youth that participated in the program by 51% (Asaro, 2019: 48). Suppose big data and machine learning is used to identify and reduce specific crime-inducing parameters, such as unemployment, poverty, social exclusion, and lack of education. In that case, some issues pertinent to offending might likely be addressed more effectively in the long run. Software engineers and developers cannot do this on their own. Artificial intelligence and machine learning need input from social sciences and humanities. It is essential to do this now, as we might not have the tools to deal with the consequences of non-engagement in the future. Another key question is not whether we can (or whether we should) make forecasts about crime and offending at all; big data and machine learning should be able to point us in the right direction, probably with more accuracy as the technology develops. The question that matters is what actions we take, based on these forecasts.

The potential commercialisation of combating future crime and offending was intentionally not included in this chapter. However, one must flag that companies that develop AI technology and automated justice tools are making large sums of money out of the business (see Wilson, 2018). There is also little transparency when it comes to an understanding of the development and deployment of such tools (Angwin et al., 2016; O'Neill, 2017). The consequences of the privatisation of prison systems in the Global North and the rise of the prison-industrial complex must be a learning curve. The fact that private companies sell products to government agencies (products that potentially have a vast impact on people's lives) with limited, if any, oversight from academia and civil society is a worrying development indeed. As such, this issue warrants immediate and comprehensive scrutiny.

Conclusion

Artificial intelligence's expansion is unlikely to slow down in the future, regardless of the prospect of AGI or technological singularity. As Toby Walsh (2017) notes, AI will ultimately be like electricity: omnipresent and invisible. Offending and crime control relevant AI applications are expected to surge in the near future; Hayward and Maas (2020) suggest a timeframe of a mere five years. The success of both delinquents and crime-fighting agencies tends to look like this; 'take X and add AI' (Kevin Kelly, cited in Chase, 2018: section 4.2). AI systems might take the role of a criminal, a detective, and a judge. While some of the above scenarios might look remote, the role AI plays in contemporary policing and criminal courts need to be carefully analysed. If anything, these developments provide a clear signal that if we remain passive or take technology for granted, things can quickly get out of hand.

One of the developers of *HunchLab*, Robert Cheetam (2019: emphasis added), recently noted that

> [m]achine learning and artificial intelligence are going to have a profound impact on our society, and the decisions we make in the next decade will affect how we live for the next century or more. We will need to find *creative, inventive ways to reconcile our values with the technology we create.*

Creativity and innovation are of the utmost importance in our engagement with AI. Researchers need to connect and bridge the divide that exists within the community, especially when it comes to the IT industry and social sciences/humanities. As Max Tegmark (2017) puts it, the challenges we face today transcend traditional boundaries between areas of expertise and nations. We need to join forces and produce the guidelines and regulations that will be implemented in the industry. To avoid future adverse outcomes, we ought to invest significant effort and resources in embedding ethics in AI agents. This is a growing area of research, but more energy is put in developing the technology rather than trying to understand and address its limitations. We need to think about how to install the following fundamental values in future AI development.

First, we ought to set the red lines that cannot be crossed and implement the Model of Care approach as a default mechanism that guides AI and machine learning advances. We need to avoid *blackboxing* by ensuring transparency of algorithms, products, and systems, and enabling oversight by stakeholders such as civil society or individuals affected by algorithm-based decisions. The AI systems in crime control must be a subject of independent scrutiny and evaluation, and we need to ensure that technology is not used as an excuse for human rights violations or further marginalisation of vulnerable populations. We also need a greater understanding of possible or likely scenarios for machine learning, and what strategies we should deploy to prevent negative outputs and outcomes that follow the application of AI systems and agents. Another important point is considering further detachment of human-thing hybrids that comes with machine learning and increasingly independent AI technology. Algorithms are, thus, companion species that might have a life of their own, without our control, and we need to think how to ensure we continue to play an essential part in a thing-human symbiosis.

We require backing from, and assistance by legal scholars in re-thinking our legal systems and responses in the fast-changing areas such as criminal liability and automated justice. Resisting some of the narratives identified above, however appealing they might be, is of critical importance if we wish to avoid mistakes in the future. There is no doubt that devices and machines are faster in processing big data, and that we should not, for example, consider going back to physical, human-operated facial recognition techniques. We should certainly not give up trying to unpack how we can harness technology in addressing issues around crime and victimisation of the future. Nevertheless, we ought to steer away from false promises—if not fairy tales—underpinned by the belief that things are impartial and less likely to error than humans. Using advanced technology does not translate into a better, more equal, and just world. By using weak AI, we know this for sure. If and when we get to the AGI, we can only speculate, with trepidation, what the outcome might be. I now turn to the Internet of things as a digital frontier technology that could assist us in answering some of these and other pressing questions.

Notes

1 Such an outcome could be a result of a deliberate act, engineering mistakes or circumstances pertinent to the environment that would lead to it. See Yampolskiy (2019).
2 Such as Marvin Minsky, John McCarthy, Ray Solomonoff, and others.
3 I decided not to use a better-known example of *PredPol* software, firstly because it is well explored in the literature, and secondly, because it did not experience such a dramatic evolution as *HunchLab*.
4 The system was bought by *ShotSpotter Law Enforcement Solutions* that aims to 'proactively address gun violence issues' by acoustic sensors deployed in major cities and automated systems alerting police about shootings (see shotspotter.com).
5 Gordon Moore, the founder of Intel, observed in 1965 that the number of transistors being placed in a chip double every year, but predicted that this trend would only last for ten years. There are indicators that Moore's law is coming to an end. This, however, is not so important given the connectivity of computers, devices, and smart machines in the future Internet. In other words, computational power is not so relevant anymore when a simple question to Siri has been sent to thousands of computers who will work together to find a solution/answer to our question (Tvede, 2020).
6 Think, for example, that annoying sound your car makes when you fail to buckle your seat belt.

References

Angwin J., Larson J., Mattu S., et al., 2016. Machine Bias. Available from: https://www.propublica.org/article/machine-bias-risk-assessments-in-criminal-sentencing (accessed 19.02.2020).

Asaro, P., 2019. AI ethics in predictive policing: from models of threat to ethics of care. IEEE Technol. Soc. Mag. 38 (2), 40–53.

Baraniuk C., 2019. The new weapon in the fight against crime. Available from: https://www.bbc.com/future/article/20190228-how-ai-is-helping-to-fight-crime (accessed 18.02.2020).

Bennett Moses, L., Chan, J., 2014. Using Big Data for legal and law enforcement decisions: testing the new tools. UNSW Law J. 37 (2), 643–678.

Bostrom, N., 2017. *Superintelligence: Paths, Dangers, Strategies.* Oxford University Press, Oxford.

Brahan, J.W., Lam, K.P., Chan, H., et al., 1998. AICAMS: artificial intelligence crime analysis and management system. Knowl. Syst. 11 (5-6), 355–361.

Broad, E., 2018. Made by Humans: The AI Condition. Melbourne University Publishing, Melbourne.

Bunz, M., Meikle, G., 2018. The Internet of Things. Polity, Cambridge and Medford.

Cellan-Jones, R., 2014. Stephen Hawking warns artificial intelligence could end mankind. BBC News, 2 December.

Chammah M., Hansen M., 2016. Policing the future. In: The Marshal Project. Available from: https://www.themarshallproject.org/2016/02/03/policing-the-future (accessed 2.12.2020).

Chase, C., 2018. Surviving AI. Three Cs, Bradford.

Cheetham R., 2019. Why we sold HunchLab. Available from: https://www.azavea.com/blog/2019/01/23/why-we-sold-hunchlab/ (accessed 14.02.2020).

Cush A., 2016. This Program That Judges Use to Predict Future Crimes Seems Racist as Hell. Available from: https://gawker.com/this-program-that-judges-use-to-predict-future-crimes-s-1778151070 (accessed 30.01.2020).

Danaylov, N., 2016. Conversations with the Future: 21 Visions for the 21st Century. Singularity Media Inc., Toronto.

EMPAC, 2017. Analytics: The digital policing revolution. Available from: http://www.empac.org.uk/analytics-digital-policing-revolution/ (accessed 2.12.2020).

Eubanks, V., 2017. Automating Inequality. St. Martin's Press, New York.

Ferguson, A.G., 2012. Predictive policing and reasonable suspicion. Emory Law J. 62, 259–325.

Floridi, L., Sanders, J.W., 2004. On the morality of artificial agents. Minds Mach. 14 (3), 349–379.

Future of Life Institute, 2020. *Benefits and Risks of Artificial Intelligence.* Available from: https://futureoflife.org/background/benefits-risks-of-artificial-intelligence/?cn-reloaded=1&cn-reloaded=1&cn-reloaded=1 (accessed 17.02.2020.).

Gent, E., 2020. Artificial intelligence is evolving all by itself. Science, 13 April.

Gerritsen, C., 2020. Big data and criminology from an AI perspective. In: Leclerc, B., Cale, J. (Eds.), Big Data. Routledge, Abingdon and New York.

Goodman, M., 2016. Future Crimes: Inside the Digital Underground and the Battle for Our Connected World. Anchor Books, New York.

Gunkel, D., 2020. How to Survive a Robot Invasion: Rights, Responsibility, and AI. Routledge, New York.

Hallevy, G., 2010. The criminal liability of artificial intelligence entities - from science fiction to legal social controL. Akron Intellect. Property J. 4 (2), 171–201.

Harari, Y.N., 2018. 21 Lessons for the 21st Century. Jonathan Cape, London.

Hawking, S., Russel, S., Tegmark, M., et al., 2014. Stephen Hawking: 'Transcendence looks at the implications of artificial intelligence – but are we taking AI seriously enough?' Available from: https://www. independent.co.uk/news/science/stephen-hawking-transcendence-looks-implications-artificial-intelligence-are-we-taking-ai-seriously-en-ough-9313474.html (accessed 30.01.2020).

Hayward, K.J., Maas, M.M., 2020. Artificial intelligence and crime: a primer for criminologists. Crime Media Cult. doi:10.1177/1741659020917434. 1741659020917434.

Hildebrandt, M., 2008. Ambient intelligence, criminal liability and democracy. Crim. Law Philos. 2 (2), 163–180.

Jennings, C., 2019. Artificial Intelligence: Rise of the Lightspeed Learners. Rowman and Littlefield, Lanham, Boulder, New York, London.

Joh, E., 2017a. Artificial intelligence and policing: first questions. Seattle Univ. Law Rev. 41, 1139–1144.

Joh, E., 2017b. Feeding the machine: policing, crime data, and algorithms. William Mary Bill. Rights J. 26 (2), 287–302.

Kaplan, J., 2016. Artificial Intelligence: What Everyone Needs to Know. Oxford University Press, Incorporated, Oxford, United States.

King, T.C., Aggarwal, N., Taddeo, M., et al., 2020. Artificial intelligence crime: an interdisciplinary analysis of foreseeable threats and solutions. Sci. Eng. Ethics 26 (1), 89–120.

Kitchin, R., 2014. The Data Revolution: Big Data, Open Data, Data Infrastructures and Their Consequences. SAGE Publications, Los Angeles, London, New Delhi, Singapore, Washington D.C.

Kobie, N., 2019. The complicated truth about China's social credit system. Wired. https://www.wired.co.uk/article/china-social-credit-system-explained (accessed 25.02.2020).

Kurzweil, R., 2005. The Singularity Is Near: When Humans Transcend Biology. Viking, New York.

Latour, B., 1999. Pandora's Hope: Essays on the Reality of Science Studies. Harvard University Press, Cambridge.

Marcus, G., Davis, E., 2020. GPT-3, Bloviator: OpenAI's language generator has no idea what it's talking about. Available from: https://www. technologyreview.com/2020/08/22/1007539/gpt3-openai-language-generator-artificial-intelligence-ai-opinion (accessed 25.02.2020).

McCulloch, J., Wilson, D., 2015. Pre-Crime: Pre-Emption, Precaution and the Future. Routledge, London, United Kingdom.

O'Neill, C., 2016. Weapons of Math Destruction: How Big Data Increases Inequality and Threatens Democracy. Penguin Books, United Kingdom.

O'Neill, C., 2017. The era of blind faith in big data must end. TED2017 (ed). TED2017.

Perry, S., Roda, C., 2016. Human Rights and Digital Technology: Digital Tightrope. Palgrave Macmillan Limited, London, United Kingdom.

Phillips, J., Hahn, C., Fontana, P., et al., 2020. Four Principles of Explainable Artificial Intelligence. Internal Report 8312. National Institute of Standards and Technology Interagency, Gaithersburg, Maryland. https://www.nist.gov/system/files/documents/2020/08/17/NIST%20Explainable%20AI%20Draft%20-NISTIR8312%20%281%29.pdf (accessed 25.02.2020).

Pichai S., 2018. AI at Google: our principles. Available from: https://blog.google/technology/ai/ai-principles/ (accessed 14.02.2020).

Revell T., 2017. AI detective analyses police data to learn how to crack cases. Available from: https://www.newscientist.com/article/mg23431254-000-ai-detective-analyses-police-data-to-learn-how-to-crack-cases/ (accessed 26.02.2020).

Rigano, C., 2019. Using artificial intelligence to address criminal justice needs. Natl. Inst. Justice J. 280, 1–10.

Russel, S., Norvig, P., 2016. Artificial Intelligence: A Modern Approach. Pearson, Harlow, UK.

Schneider, S., 2019. Artificial You: AI and the Future of Your Mind. Princeton University Press, Princeton and Oxford.

Shapiro, A., 2017. Reform predictive policing. Nature 541 (541), 458–460.

Slijper, F., 2019. Reprogramming War. I. PAX, Utrecht.

Tegmark, M., 2017. Life 3.0: Being Human in the Age of Artificial Intelligence. Penguin Books Limited, United Kingdom.

Tvede, L., 2020. Supertrends: 50 Things You Need to Know about the Future. John Wiley & Sons, Incorporated, Newark.

United Nations, 2018. World Economic and Social Survey 2018: Frontier technologies for sustainable development.

Verbeek, P.-P., 2011. Moralizing Technology: Understanding and Designing the Morality of Things. University of Chicago Press, Chicago, United States.

Walsh, T., 2017. It's Alive!: Artificial Intelligence from the Logic Piano to Killer Robots. La Trobe University Press, in conjunction with Black Incorporated, Melbourne.

Wilson, D., 2018. Algorithmic patrol: the future of predictive policing. In: Završnik, A. (Ed.), Big data, crime and social control. Routledge, London and New York.

Yampolskiy, R., 2019. Preface: introduction to AI safety and security. In: Yampolskiy, R. (Ed.), Artificial Intelligence Safety and Security. CRC Press, Boca Raton, London, New York.

Završnik, A., 2018. Big data: What is it and why does it matter for crime and social control? In: Završnik, A. (Ed.), Big Data, Crime and Social Control. Routledge, London and New York.

4

'THE INTERNET OF EVERYTHING'

Techno-social hybrids of the internet of things[1]

Introduction

Remember the scenarios from the beginning of this book? While some of the mentioned situations might materialise in the future, many elements of the Fourth Industrial Revolution are now a reality. Networks of interconnected smart devices are growing, while engagement with these ground-breaking innovations in social sciences remains limited at best. From humble beginnings in the late 1980s, when only about 100,000 hosts were connected to the Internet (Baras and Brito, 2018), the world we now live in is fundamentally changed by the Internet of things. One of the very first examples of the technology that connects ordinary objects to the Internet was a Coca-Cola vending machine located at Carnegie Mellon University. In 1982, programmers working at the university's IT department decided it would be great to contact the machine and check the stocktake before making a long trip for refreshment—so they wrote a software that did just that (Foote, 2016; Tvede, 2020). Kevin Ashton from the Massachusetts Institute of Technology coined the expression 'the Internet of things' in the late 1990s to describe a network of objects connected to the Internet, and one another (Claveria, 2019). In 2008, the number of devices connected to the Internet surpassed the world's population (Baras and Brito, 2018). This development continues at pace: some projections state that by the year 2032, an individual will be connected to 3,000 to 5,000 things (Barrett, 2012). While we should take such projections with caution, the annual growth rate in the number of the IoT devices as of 2020 is 15-20% (Tvede, 2020). This development has led to suggestions that, in the future, '[e]verything from tyres to toothbrushes will fall within communications range, heralding the dawn of a new era' (International Telecommunications Union, 2005: 1) of 'Internet of Everything' (Greengard, 2015).

Connected smart devices, as it will be explored in this chapter, do not merely reply to stimuli (i.e. it is cold in the house, turn up the heating); they create data and communicate, prompting actions within networks. Like the analysis in the previous chapter, and having in mind the scarcity of the literature, this chapter does not purport to offer an all-encompassing theoretical account of the IoT in criminology. It also does not strive to answer the many legal, ethical, and political questions raised when pondering these technologies in a criminological context. What this chapter seeks to do is to start the conversation. The focus here is exclusively on the IoT systems, while other advances associated with it, such as facial recognition technology, are only lightly touched upon.

The chapter commences with the definition(s) of the IoT, followed by the debate on privacy and data security, the 'Internet of evidence', and the future of offending. A particular emphasis is placed on the development of 'smart homes' and 'smart cities', and exploration of how technology may lead to 'smart borders'. The chapter also offers a brief look at how the IoT can further marginalise the Other, in particular people with limited mobility potential and populations already subject to extensive surveillance and control. The final segment provides some theoretical insights on the matter, where I propose theoretical frameworks we could use to respond to identified challenges.

Unpacking the wonderworld of the IoT

While there is no universal definition of the IoT, one of the most practical definitions is by Bunz and Meikle (2018) who suggest that IoT systems are many uses and processes that stem from giving a network address to a thing and fitting it with sensors. The following common elements are present in the IoT: it is a *network* of objects, with *unique identity* (unique identification number and Internet Protocol address), small *power supplies, sensors* (with sensing/actuation capability that can capture context and provide information about the thing itself or its environment), and *connection*—the ability to communicate with one another and transmit and receive data (Howard, 2015: xi). The objects are often, but not always, characterised by *a higher degree of computational, analytical, and action abilities* (Burgess, 2018). As they get connected to one another and the environment, they gain new capabilities or skills such as seeing, speaking, or tracing (Bunz and Meikle, 2018). New skills of smart devices—or ambient intelligence as the IoT is also referred to (see Chase, 2018)—increasingly include decision-making or action, with little or no human input.

For the purpose of this chapter, the IoT is defined as 'a variety of things or objects ... which, through unique addressing schemes, are able to interact with each other, and *cooperate with their neighbors to reach common goals*' (Atzori et al., 2010: 2787; emphasis added). Things in the IoT network have several layers of connection. Sensing technology such as RFID tags, intelligent sensors, and RFID readers comprise the lower layer. The middle (network) and upper (service) layers are networked systems that enable communication and connection between things, such as cloud internetwork (social and mobile networks, WLAN). The application-interface layer is where interaction and activity occur—in smart cities, power grids, and transportation control systems (Li, 2017). Smart devices in the IoT networks can be changed or altered from anywhere, by anything, ideally with little to no human intervention (Baras and Brito, 2018; Tuptuk and Hailes, 2019). Most networks in operation today are centralised; a client-server network. In other words, communication that happens between objects goes through the central server (Hossain, 2020). In the future Internet, this might not be the case, as networks are likely to be decentralised. As such, humans might be unaware of the sense and exchange of data between objects, or where the data is stored. Those of us aware of what is going on, as argued later, will unlikely opt-out of things-run surveillance networks. Critically, connected objects will have the ability to configure themselves autonomously, adapt to change, and take action, powered by AI algorithms.

It is essential at this point to outline the typology of things in the IoT networks. They are indeed diverse; some are physical-first, meaning that they generate or exchange data only when augmented or manipulated, such as desks or chairs. Others are digital-first, specifically designed to generate and exchange data, for example smartphones (Greengard, 2015. 16) Connected things can be physical (i.e. physical objects) or virtual (i.e. software, code). Finally, there is a distinction between conventional IoT that require human involvement and analysis (such as connected contact lenses that send information to your doctor for diagnosis), and the autonomous IoT that have the capacity to bypass humans (for example, the autonomous self-healing systems used in manufacturing that can predict and repair things without human participation). Autonomous IoT are examples of the intersection of the IoT and AI, in which objects make sense of data, learn from it and one another, and change its performance. All the above-mentioned types of the IoT technology (other than software/code analysed in Chapter 3) are examined in this chapter.

Scanning and scenario writing: The surge and impact of smart devices

The future Internet is often described as a smart environment (Gubbi et al., 2013), where technology will transform our bodies, homes, transport systems, workplaces, communities, and nation-states. Many areas of social life apply a range of IoT technology, especially in what is now known as 'smart cities'. Baig et al. (2017: 3) describe a smart city as a 'connected environment for all its citizens ... [whose] services can extend into many diverse domains including the environment, transportation, health, tourism, home energy management, and safety and security'. In smart cities, regulation of water, electricity, waste, traffic, and parking is gradually transferred from humans to the networked objects. Homes and buildings with automated lighting, heating, energy consumption, and greenhouse production are at the forefront of the ambient intelligence (Baras and Brito, 2018). Healthcare, energy sectors, and transportation are also areas where the IoT is breaking new ground as it enables doctors to monitor elderly patients in their homes, reducing hospitalisation costs through early intervention (Gubbi et al., 2013). While the impact of the IoT has been the topic of science and technology literature for quite some time now, questions pertinent to ambient intelligence and offending, as well as its social applications, remain largely unanswered. Existing literature mainly focuses on cybercrime and risk of potential attacks on the IoT network (Gubbi et al., 2013; Greengard, 2015; Baig et al., 2017; Tuptuk and Hailes, 2019). This focus indicates the need for research in social sciences that pivots both on risks and vulnerabilities the future Internet brings, but also on how technology can assist in addressing various crime and human rights concerns, such as the right to privacy.

Who is watching who?: Ubiquitous surveillance, security, privacy, and agency in the era of the IoT

Contemporary surveillance, as suggested in Chapter 2, is called ubiquitous to depict the ambient in which it is difficult, if not impossible, to 'opt-out'. Surveillance is also ongoing: computers, smartphones, and other smart devices continuously collect and share information about our activities. Physical and digital-first objects that sense and share information about and around us 'could be the most effective mass surveillance infrastructure we've ever built' (Howard, 2015: xvii). In the IoT, there is no tall towers with omnipresent guards Jeremy Bentham envisioned in his utopian prison design, nor is it a self-discipline surveillance and control system defined by Foucault. This theme will be elaborated in the final section of this chapter. For now, it is important to note that the IoT innovations have been marketed as necessary, a must-have technology that will improve the quality of our lives. The IoT arguably facilitates 'a convenient way … to keep an eye on the inside and outside of [our] homes from any location with internet access' (Dixon, 2017: 37; see also Weber, 2017).

As we keep an eye on possessions and properties, our little helpers relentlessly monitor and exchange information about us, often inconspicuously. They send data to manufacturers, developers, and other agencies that use them for a variety of commercial and non-commercial purposes. As Andrew Guthrie Ferguson would have it, '[w]e are now all living with little smart spies in our houses' (CBC Radio, 2018). Amazon's Alexa or Google Home's Smart Speaker monitor movements, listen to voice commands, and record events even when you switch them off. Amazon's Ring can let the police see footage from your front porch. Surveillance in the IoT is pervasive, conducted by many different things, a super-sized version of 'surveillant assemblage' (Haggerty and Ericson, 2000). It is performed through the continuous process of data gathering via many sensors in the IoT systems, sent to the central server(s) for processing, analysing, and actioning in a response to the input.

A range of actors (governments, businesses, military-industrial complex and private enterprises) aspire to surveil and manipulate people's behaviour via the IoT (see Howard, 2015). Indeed, surveillance *per definitionem* is 'the focused, systematic and routine attention to personal details for purposes of influence, management, protection or direction' (Lyon, 2007: 14). In the IoT, surveillance is so omnipresent that privacy emerges as the critical issue; more specifically, the right to be let alone (Warren and Brandeis, cited in Bunz and Meikle, 2018: 123). An abundance of literature explores privacy concerns in relation to the IoT (Williams, 2016; Claypoole, 2016; Goodman, 2016; Baig et al., 2017; Dixon, 2017), while some recent smart city experiments failed because of privacy breaches (Johnston, 2020). The European Commission on the IoT governance recently recommended that developers adopt 'privacy by design' approach when fostering new IoT systems (Vos, 2018). While some of us might be alarmed by the prospect of ever-expanding data sharing, our desire for smart things is likely to prevail. We will, therefore, get Alexa or Google Home, a self-driving car, or that spying smart chair because they offer 'status, approval, enjoyment' (Lyon, 2018: 82). Privacy, as a concept, is likely to experience substantial changes in the future Internet. What should be of interest to social scientists, however, is not just the extent of surveillance per se, but who has access to data, and what legal frameworks we need to design to address issues that might emerge in decades to come.

One of the most discussed concerns in the IoT literature and public discourse is that large networks of connected things could be open to potential hacks (Roman et al., 2011; Gubbi et al., 2013; Claypoole, 2016; DeNisco Rayome, 2017). As such, 'each connected device could be a potential doorway into the IoT infrastructure or personal data' (Li, 2017: 2; 4). While some of these security intrusions are indeed disturbing[2], other issues with duplicitous attributes could become more pressing. Let us use a common (and often mocked) case study in the IoT analysis: a smart fridge. A local bottle shop is likely to deliver your favourite beer as requested by a smart fridge when the supply run out. The benefit of convenience, however, could be offset if the fridge overrules your recent decision to quit drinking. Or, consider a serious ethical dilemma smart car developers face when embedding algorithms that will have the power to decide whom to 'sacrifice' in a case of an emergency (Bonnefon et al., 2016: this issue will be explored in Chapter 5). Automated objects around us share and evaluate data, but also make decisions on our behalf. In contrast, humans' preference on the matter—for example, whether or not we would like particular information to be shared with our doctors, employers, government, or family members, or the decision to give up drinking—becomes irrelevant. Smart things become sole actants, with goals misaligned with those of humans. The impact of the IoT technology on our agency and autonomy is one of the many challenges social scientists, lawyers, and criminologists will face in the future.

From 'crime harvest' to 'the Internet of evidence': Offending and solving crimes in smart environments

While the literature offers an insightful overview of ethical debates pertinent to ambient intelligence, somewhat absent from these discussions is the potential use of the IoT systems in committing and solving crimes. Samuel Greengard (2015: xv) suggests that the technology and in particular the IoT, 'will affect everything from the way people vote to the way we eat at restaurants and take vacations', and that 'the future could introduce new types of crime, weapons, and warfare'. Some end-users and commentators have called the IoT technology 'a security disaster waiting to happen' (CompTia, 2016: 3) and impending 'crime harvest' (Palmer, 2018). If, as described above, lifelines such as energy, healthcare, transportation, and even our bodies are all on a mega-grid, the issue of disrupting the grid becomes a major concern. A malfunction or interruption of the future Internet could potentially impact a large proportion of the population, from financial institutions and hospitals, to public transport and distribution of goods. Denial of Service (DoS) and the more sinister Distributed Denial of Service (DDoS) or Ransom Denial of Service (RDoS) attacks that aim to restrict or deny access to services are already a major headache for developers, early adopters and consumers, corporate executives, and governments (DeNisco Rayome, 2017; for a range of potential scenarios see Tzezana, 2016; Tuptuk and Hailes, 2019). Most concerningly, the human body itself could be hacked through the IoT (Ashton, 2017; Goodman, 2016) via pacemakers or medical implants. In 2013, former US Vice President Dick Cheney disclosed that doctors deactivated wireless function on his heart implant to prevent a potential terrorist attack (Tuptuk and Hailes, 2019). As Marc Goodman, founder of the Future Crimes Institute explains (cited in Chabinsky, 2015), '[w]hen your heart is online for your doctor to access, it is also available to the kid next door. … For the first time in human history, the human body itself has become susceptible to cyber attack'.

Warnings that legal systems and crime control agencies need to 'catch up' with technology have also been revived (Ashton, 2017), as there is 'no doubt that, in the future, ambient intelligence will be handy in solving crimes' (Alohali, 2017: 177; see also Kearns, 2018). Law enforcement agencies across the Global North have been increasingly using the IoT technology in their daily activities. An example is the Los Angeles Police Department's Real-Time Analysis Critical Response Division (detailed in Ferguson, 2017), or the 'first-ever smart patrol car system that fully integrates video captured from in-car and body-worn cameras' (Ives, 2015: 2; Zimmer, 2017). Ambient intelligence in smart cities will assist in building maintenance and repair, waste and traffic management, pollution monitoring and regulation, and smart lighting (Zanella et al., 2014), but also in crime prevention (if not pre-emption) and investigation. Sensing devices will track the movement of pedestrians in dark streets, turn on street lighting and cameras when needed, and send data to police for processing (Lee, 2015). Machine learning-enabled video cameras could also help a potential victim detect, in milliseconds, whether a purported robber holds a real gun or not, and alert law enforcement if the former is confirmed (TEDx Talks, 2018). Finally, sensing devices mounted on street lamps and other infrastructure have been used by law enforcement in some cities in the US to detect and respond to gunfire (Electronic Frontier Foundation, 2020). As devices for sensing, detecting, and data transmission become mainstream, human decision-making in policing might soon become redundant:

> An illicit driver enters a smart city attempting to subvert all policing controls in place for traffic regulation. The driven vehicle enters the city and increases speed past the stipulated limit … an incident response team will be alerted immediately by sensory data which is transmitted over to the centralized Cloud and measured as being anomalous by the relevant data analysis engine. Subsequently, the traffic control authority (the police) will be alerted with the data emerging from the Cloud, and necessary tactical action will be taken to control the incident.
>
> *(Baig et al., 2017: 10)*

Similar to advances outlined in the previous chapter, in the IoT-run smart cities, humans might not control whether data is sent to other devices or the cloud, and the thing-human alliance might slowly diminish to give way to thing-only systems. The IoT devices will become a novel type of companion species that will have a life of their own but will also make decisions about our lives and crimes.

The IoT technology has many applications in criminal courts. In the United States, judge Dixon (2017) identified various contexts where smart home evidence collected via networked ambient intelligence has been presented in the court of law. Orr and Sanchez (2018) investigated a case where police in the US state of Arkansas presented Amazon with a warrant for recorded voice data stored on an Amazon server, after collecting the device from a murder suspect. They concluded that smart AI-powered IoT devices, in particular Amazon Echo and Alexa, can provide valuable legal evidence in criminal justice proceedings. In '"the Internet of evidence" … smart devices are going to show up in criminal prosecutions' (Andrew Guthrie Ferguson, cited in CBC Radio, 2018), often to testify against their owners. Their reach and impact, however, is not limited to smart homes or smart cities of the future.

'Smart borders': Sensing and regulating mobility

Contemporary states seem to embrace two outwardly juxtaposed developments in bordering practices that aim to combat illegalised migration: erection of border walls and fences, and development of tech-based border security interventions. Technology has been at the forefront of governing migration and mobility for several decades. As such, a range of security technologies (Neal, 2009; Milivojevic, 2013; Milivojevic, 2019a)—technology-human interconnections developed to do just that—have been developed and applied in the Global North and Global South. They comprise of strategies, policies, hardware, and software that aim to strengthen borders and regulate the flow of citizens, non-citizens, goods, and trade (see Koslowski, 2004; Brouwer, 2008; Cote-Boucher, 2008; Ceyhan, 2008; Broeders and Hampshire, 2013; Popescu, 2015). Surveillance of mobile populations is emerging as a preferred method of consolidating risky borderlands. As Adey (2012: 193) accurately points out, 'borders are married to the practice and evolution of surveillance'. Countries of origin and transit have emerged as principal sites for the detection, surveillance, and classification of border crossers. The goal is to 'check individuals as far from [the nation state] as possible and through each part of their journey' (UK Cabinet Office, cited in Vaughan-Williams, 2010: 1073). The contemporary 'biometric state' has an 'almost obsessive preoccupation with where you are going and who you are' (Muller, 2010: 8).

In times of increased mobility, however, conventional security measures that require human decision-making struggle to process and respond to big data produced by and about (legalised and illegalised) border crossers. High-tech checkpoints equipped with scanners, security cameras, and screening systems are staffed with security personnel, who still must check and verify numerous passports, and monitor the border via thermal imaging cameras. Border guards, thus, decide on incoming travellers' rights to enter the country and act to intercept 'illegal' migrants. The IoT systems are likely to augment this process in two critical ways, and, in doing so, further extend the border by screening mobile bodies before they board planes, ships, and cars. First, the IoT technology that carries, or is carried, worn, or embedded into bodies of border crossers (such as smart blood sugar devices or nanobots injected into the bloodstream) leaves a digital trail that can be read and used to regulate their migratory projects. Technology will sensor and transmit data about people's movements: where they are, who they are meeting or travelling with, what trajectory they intend to take, and what their body temperature and heartbeat is. 'Risky' individuals could be identified at arm's length, while desired travellers will be acknowledged as such well before they reach the physical border. As people embark on a journey across state borders, information about their plans and activities will be sent to other non-human actors in the network, making it harder to engage in covert cross-border activity. Another way in which smart devices are likely to change border control is linked to the fact that security technologies deployed at the border and beyond will be more autonomous in their operation. The IoT could thereby advance 'futuristic and high-tech security fantasies' (Adey, 2012: 193) of pervasive, seamless borders that segregate wanted from unwanted mobility. While the 'digital divide' as uneven access and distribution of these technologies is the factor to have in mind when discussing technology and mobility (Milivojevic, 2019b; Dekker and Engbersen, 2014), the seamless IoT borders are undoubtedly in the making.

In the pursuit of security, a justification for new technological hybrids at the border and beyond will be the need to detect and immobilise people smugglers, human traffickers, and illegalised border crossers before they approach physical borders. Non-citizens or visa over-stayers could also be detected automatically in hospitals, classrooms, or workplaces, and border security officials tipped off as to their location. Secure and entirely digitised smart borders will enable the passage and the right to stay for *the right number* of *the right people* (Milivojevic, 2019a): the 'risky', 'dangerous' or unproductive border crossers will be kept at a safe distance, or as demonstrated below—singled out from within.

Intersectionalities: Targeting the 'Other'

In 2015, Google rolled out a new AI-powered feature for its Photo app that analysed photos by tagging them as 'beaches', 'cities', 'animals', and 'people'. After a few months, following a notorious incident where Google Photos labelled a woman of colour as 'gorilla' (see Bunz and Meikle, 2018: 90–91), Google admitted it failed to optimise its app for people with black skin. Occasionally, neural networks that underpin AI learning and computational process fail. While this is not strictly an example of the IoT technology, we can draw an analogy: objects networked in the IoT 'see', but their vision might be somewhat limited. If there is an unfair bias towards accurately mapping and recognising a normative standard for facial structure—as seen in a white 'norm' example in above-mentioned 'gorilla' incident—then does the software embedded in the IoT also risk homogenising 'Others' and unfairly discriminating by potentially labelling them as threats, at a greater frequency? Certainly, as Lyon et al. (2012) argue and as suggested in this chapter, contemporary surveillance captures everyone, including groups that historically managed to avoid such scrutiny. However, as Lyon et al. continue, this often translates into new asymmetries, in which those in the position of power emerge more powerful, while marginalised end up being over-surveilled. Ubiquitous surveillance often reinforces and exacerbates existing inequalities. It is, therefore, worth exploring whether marginalised communities such as refugees, asylum seekers, ethnic and racial minorities, and former colonised subjects are more likely to be unfairly targeted by the development and deployment of the IoT. As Simone Browne (2012) powerfully demonstrates, racialised surveillance is alive and kicking, and there is a claim that the IoT systems are likely to make matters worse, given that surveillance is always accompanied, if not inspired, by social sorting (Lyon, 2018).

Some of these fault lines are already visible. As Andrejevic (2012: 94) suggests, 'relatively affluent groups and places are subject to more comprehensive forms of commercial monitoring, whereas less affluent groups and places are targeted by policing and security-oriented forms of monitoring'. The implications of these diverse forms of surveillance are clear: as a white upper-middle-class female, I will be targeted by advertisers; a woman of colour is likely to be targeted by agencies of crime control. Means Coleman and Brunton (2016) assert that this type of technological institutionalisation of social inequality is evidenced by over-policing and disproportionately high surveillance measures deployed in impoverished African American neighbourhoods. Through the IoT, socially stigmatised 'Other' could be not just over-surveilled but also discriminated against. Examples such as using data from the IoT as grounds for prevention of exit, visa revocation, or denial of services established before people's application for travel, visa, or asylum is finalised are not far-fetched. The IoT systems have the potential to monitor those deemed 'risky' at all times as they go about their day-to-day lives. As such, the technology can unfairly discriminate populations labelled as 'deviant' by way of race, ethnicity, religion, and social status, and, therefore, considered 'inherently inclined' towards criminal or anti-social behaviour.

The technological unconscious of the IoT: Theorising smart devices

Further development of ambient intelligence will not bring things to life; however, it will significantly change the dynamic between humans and networked objects. As I demonstrate above, smart things have their own 'language', use tools, and exhibit social behaviour and as such, constitute our companion species (Haraway and Wolfe, 2016). Networked things sense, track, send information, and often exclude us from exercising agency. The fact that things have agency is not new. From Heidegger to Latour, scholars have analysed the active role of things in social life. What is new with the development of the IoT is just how much agency remains for humans, and whether the equilibrium in the thing–human alliance has irrevocably shifted. While this is a principal question for philosophers, ethicists, and sociologists, criminology has to join the debate as such developments will inevitably impact on crime prevention, offending, policing, and legal and penal policies. Theorising the IoT, however, is a complex exercise. I begin with analysing the breakdown in human–thing hybrids, and its importance in understanding offending and crime control.

Given the centrality of the panopticon in social sciences and emergence of surveillance in criminological theory, we ought to use this concept as a starting point in theorising the IoT. The panopticon, as defined by Jeremy Bentham, is an institution of control where those watched regulate their own behaviour regardless of whether they are actually watched. Building on this, Foucault (2002: 70) defines panopticism as,

> a type of power that is applied to individuals in the form of continuous individual supervision, in the form of control, punishment and compensation, and in the form of correction, that is, the modelling and transforming of individuals in terms of certain norms.

However, for many scholars, the 'mere mention of the panopticon elicits exasperated groans' (Bauman and Lyon, 2013: 49) as this concept of the past is perceived as incapable of capturing the nuances of new technologies (Haggerty and Ericson, 2000; Lianos, 2003). At the turn of the century, Haggerty and Ericson (2000) proposed the notion of 'surveillant assemblage' to describe a multitude of networked devices that collect, extract, sort, analyse, and deliver information. Smart things in the IoT systems, however, not only collect data and surveil the object of surveillance; they manipulate data within these increasingly diffused, dispersed digital networks, and create action.

Sensing devices are mediators; they constitute our reality, but the outcome occasionally does not correspond to the input. The automated communication between things is a big 'part of how we live, but not a part of our day-to-day conscious existence' (Beer, 2009: 988). Ambient intelligence is an example of technology that sinks 'into its taken-for-granted background' (Thrift, 2005: 153), unobserved and unchallenged. In new media studies, this phenomenon is described as 'the technological unconscious' (Thrift, 2004; Beer, 2009; Wood, 2016). Technology runs so opaquely that we do not notice it until it fails. The IoT offers a platform for the ubiquitous ecosystem and within it, omnipresent surveillance in which we will be continuously observed by a multitude of connected things that collect, exchange, and analyse data about us. The objects sense, learn, adapt, and take action pertinent to our health and wellbeing, transportation, mobility, and energy consumption. Smart things will become the same as clothes or shoes: we will use them, convinced they would improve our quality of life or the planet. A multitude of automated, networked processes will replace the subtle coercion of self-governing panopticon and ultimately produce unconscious obedience of subjects of surveillance. While we are likely to be aware of some of its aspects, average citizens might never truly grasp the extent or the depth of this web. Smart things will be so embedded into our daily lives that we will either consider such intrusion 'normal' or will not care enough to sacrifice our preferred use of these technologies—and as such, will *comply* with it.

The utilitarianism-inspired idea of 'improved' human wellbeing underpins actions taken by the automated IoT: we might not want to look after our health, but the things will do it for us. They will be irresistible, marketed to us as objects that will improve our lives through an abundance of quantifiable data. Ultimately, however, and similar to Bentham's or Foucault's models, our behaviour will be modified, and not by force. We will be *obedient*, but not necessarily because we decide to do so. Our doctor will know about issues we have with body weight and is likely to prescribe diet and medications, but not because we finally booked that long-overdue annual check-up; it will be our Fitbit or an armchair that will blow the whistle. Our lives will be transformed, modified, just as Foucault argued surveillance would do through technologies of the self, but this time not (only) at our own volition. The societies of control (Deleuze, 1992) will materialise as an ongoing, never-ending 'self-improvement'. Finally, there is a potential for the underclass—those already marginalised, over-policed, excluded and silenced—to be disproportionately targeted in the future Internet.

There will be limited self-discipline or agency: automated things will take actions on our behalf. In the panopticon, surveillance was limited to contained, physical spaces and conducted by humans; this is not going to be the case with ambient intelligence. Indeed, it will be assemblages of things that function together as an entity (Haggerty and Ericson, 2000) that will collect, exchange, and analyse data about us. Crime prevention, offending, and punishment will happen in smart homes, cities, and states, and everyone will be a target of surveillance. An individual travelling from home to the workplace will be monitored without prior fiding of criminality or illegality, regardless of citizenship and other personal identifiers. Simply existing in a space located in a particular socio-historical context will be the justification for surveillance. The IoT technology will be everywhere: in bodies, on bodies, and around bodies, while never actually being controlled or exercised by bodies.

As smart things communicate amongst themselves and make autonomous actions without human input, there may emerge a dynamic wherein *no* member of society can ever comprehensively see how the IoT function. Surveillance and data exchange will occur in the air, as devices communicate in strings of code indecipherable to all but the most highly specialised technology specialists. The sheer quantity of information transmitted is likely to grow too massive even for these select, highly specialised humans. The technology which surveils humanity will also be, in turn, insurveilable *by* humanity. Importantly for criminologists, these processes will have an impact on criminal accountability of future offenders. Privacy, as 'the control we have over information about ourselves' (Fried, 1968: 475), will be fundamentally distorted. Ultimately, we might be so dependent on things that turning them off would amount to suicide (Joy, 2019). It is for all these reasons that we can no longer ignore the development of the IoT. The time has come for clear human-thing protocols that will articulate the circumstances in which humans are responsible for devices' behaviour (Perry and Roda, 2016) and our place in the thing-human alliance of the future.

Conclusion

Historically, having access to and control over technology translated to having power (McGuire, 2012); today, leading technology and access to data mean political, economic, and military supremacy. Political power, for example, is likely to become more concentrated in technology through the IoT and become less dependent on territory itself (Howard, 2015). Similarly, businesses that sell smart things will be even more empowered; through access to data about us they can choose to share it, or not, for profit. This may, in turn, lead to a new era in which ambient intelligence will become inevitable and unavoidable, and social scientists would be wise to consider the potential consequences that existing technology can have if or when it becomes more prevalent in the future. While the use of the IoT for commercial or state surveillance purposes was not addressed in this chapter, this issue must be tackled soon. As the report from the American Civil Liberties Union noted,

> There's simply no way to forecast how these immense powers – disproportionately accumulating in the hands of corporations seeking financial advantage and governments craving ever more control – will be used. Chances are big data and the Internet of things will make it harder for us to control our own lives, as we grow increasingly transparent to powerful corporations and government institutions that are becoming more opaque to us.
>
> *(Crump and Harwood, 2014)*

The IoT revolution could well lead into what Yuval Noah Harari (2018) calls 'human irrelevance' and create 'the useless class' of Homo sapiens. As Joy (2019) warns, 'the human race might easily permit itself to drift into a position of such dependence on the machines that it would have no practical choice but to accept all of the machine's decisions'. Importantly, it is 'much harder to struggle against irrelevance than against exploitation' (Harari, 2018: 6). While technological determinism is not the way to go, one has to agree with Greengard (2015: xv) who noted that it is impossible to know where the IoT is going to take us. Whether we agree with Goodman (2016: 39) who suggested that 'we have entrusted the backbone of civilization to machines', there is no doubt the IoT systems will shape the way humans and things act and engage with crime in the twenty-first century.

Just how much this technology is going to impact on crime and offending, as well as crime-fighting, is hard to predict. However, smart things are already featured as witnesses in criminal trials, police detectives, and assistant border guards. It is likely, that '[t]he crime scene of tomorrow is going to be the IoT' (Kearns, 2018). Criminologists and social scientists need to be proactive and contest issues at hand, however 'inevitable' they might appear. Surveillance by smart things ought to have limits and should have 'opt-in' rather than 'opt-out' design. We need to know who has access to our data, and for what purpose. As things become mediators and actants, we need to advance the debate around agency and the importance of humans in the techno-social alliance. We need to resist unlikely scenarios such as 'crime harvest' but be wary about the technological advances and how offenders could misuse them. Finally, we need to be aware of the disproportionate impact the IoT technology is likely to have on a range of Other (refugees, asylum seekers, undocumented workers, racial minorities) and contemplate and build mechanisms that will mitigate, if not eliminate, such impact.

Notes

1 This chapter is a modified and updated version of an article published with Elizabeth Radulski. I thank the publisher for permission to use it here (Milivojevic and Radulski, 2020).
2 For example, incidents where hackers broke into baby monitoring systems and talked to at least one sleeping baby (Greengard, 2015).

References

Adey, P., 2012. Borders, identification and surveillance: New regimes of border control. In: Ball, K., Haggerty, K., Lyon, D. (Eds.), Routledge Handbook of Surveillance Studies. Routledge, London and New York.

Alohali, B., 2017. Detection protocol of possible crime scenes using Internet of Things (IoT). In: Moore, M. (Ed.), Cybersecurity Breaches and Issues Surrounding Online Threat Protection. IGI Global, Hershey, Pennsylvania, pp. 175–196.

Andrejevic, M., 2012. Ubiquitous surveillance. In: Ball, K., Haggerty, K., Lyon, D. (Eds.), The Routledge Handbook of Surveillance Studies. Routledge, Abingdon Oxon, pp. 91–98.

Ashton, M., 2017. Debugging the real world: Robust criminal prosecution in the Internet of Things. Ariz. Law Rev. 59 (3), 805–835.

Atzori, L., Iera, A., Morabito, G., 2010. The Internet of Things: A survey. Comp. Netw. 54 (15), 2787–2805.

Baig, Z.A., Szewczyk, P., Valli, C., et al., 2017. Future challenges for smart cities: Cyber-security and digital forensics. Digit. Invest. 22, 3–13.

Baras, K., Brito, L., 2018. Introduction to the Internet of Things. In: Hassan, Q., ur Rehman Khan, A., Madani, S. (Eds.), Internet of Things: Challenges, Advances, Applications. CRC Press, Bocca Raton, London, New York, pp. 3–32.

Barrett, J., 2012. The Internet of Things. *TEDxCIT.* Tedx Talks You Tube. Available from: https://www.youtube.com/watch?v=QaTIt1C5R-M (accessed 10.09.2020).

Bauman, Z., Lyon, D., 2013. Liquid Surveillance. Polity, Cambridge.

Beer, D., 2009. Power through the algorithm? Participatory web cultures and the technological unconscious. N. Media Soc. 11 (6), 985–1002.

Bonnefon, J.-F., Shariff, A., Rahwan, I., 2016. The social dilemma of autonomous vehicles. Science 352 (6293), 1573–1576.

Broeders, D., Hampshire, J., 2013. Dreaming of seamless borders: ICTs and the pre-emptive governance of mobility in Europe. J. Ethnic Migr. Stud. 39 (8), 1201–1218.

Brouwer, E., 2008. Digital Borders and Real Rights: Effective Remedies for Third-Country Nationals in the Schengen Information System. Martinus Nijhoff Publishers, Leiden.

Browne, S., 2012. Race and surveillance. In: Ball, K., Haggerty, K., Lyon, D. (Eds.), Routledge Handbook of Surveillance Studies. Routledge, London and New York, pp. 72–79.

Bunz, M., Meikle, G., 2018. The Internet of Things. Polity, Cambridge and Medford.

Burgess, M. 2018 What is the Internet of Things? WIRED explains. Wired, 16 February.

CBC Radio, 2018. "Alexa, who did it?": What happens when a judge in a murder trial wants data from a smart home speaker. Available from: https://www.cbc.ca/radio/day6/alexa-who-did-it-what-happens-when-a-judge-in-a-murder-trial-wants-the-data-from-a-smart-home-speaker-1.4916556?fbclid=IwAR0fBKs XEanePMcs-7ejyqhX5--_uXcTsM0IetjnFO9WSaZkzcrnqm00Kxg (accessed 11.09.2019).

Ceyhan, A., 2008. Technologization of security: Management of uncertainty and risk in the age of biometrics. Surveill. Soc. 5 (2), 102–123.

Chabinsky S., 2015. What does the future of cyber crime hold for you? Available from: https://www.securitymagazine.com/articles/86135-what-does-the-future-of-cyber-crime-hold-for-you (accessed 11.09).

Chase, C., 2018. Surviving AI. Three Cs, Bradford.

Claveria K., 2019. Meet Kevin Ashton, the visionary technologist who named the Internet of Things. Available from: https://www.visioncritical.com/blog/kevin-ashton-internet-of-things (accessed 02.06.2020).

Claypoole, T., 2016. Smarter Devices = More Vulnerability to Government and Criminals. Comput. Internet Lawyer 33 (11), 1–5.

CompTia, 2016. Internet of Things and opportunities. https://www.comptia.org/content/research/internet-of-things-insights-and-opportunities (accessed 02.06.2020).

Cote-Boucher, K., 2008. The diffuse border: Intelligence-sharing, control and confinement along Canada's 'Smart Border'. Surveill. Soc. 5 (2), 142–165.

Crump C., Harwood M., 2014. Invasion of the Data Snatchers: Big Data and the Internet of Things Means the Surveillance of Everything. Available from:

https://www.aclu.org/blog/speakeasy/invasion-data-snatchers-big-data-and-internet-things-means-surveillance-everything (accessed 11.09.2020).

Dekker, R., Engbersen, G., 2014. How social media transform migrant networks and facilitate migration. Glob. Netw. 14 (4), 401–418.

Deleuze, G., 1992. Postscript on the societies of control. October 59, 3–7.

DeNisco Rayome A., 2017. DDoS attacks increased 91% in 2017 thanks to IoT. Available from: https://www.techrepublic.com/article/ddos-attacks-increased-91-in-2017-thanks-to-iot/ (accessed 11.09.2020).

Dixon, H., 2017. The wonderful and scary Internet of Things! Judges J. 56 (3), 36–38.

Electronic Frontier Foundation, 2020. Acoustic gunshot detection. Available from: https://www.eff.org/pages/gunshot-detection (accessed 3.09.2020).

Ferguson, A.G., 2017. The Rise of Big Data Policing: Surveillance, Race, and the Future of Law Enforcement. New York University Press, New York.

Foote K., 2016. A Brief History of the Internet of Things. Available from: https://www.dataversity.net/brief-history-internet-things/ (accessed 13.09.2020).

Foucault, M., 2002. Power: Essential Works of Foucault 1954–1984. Penguin Books, London.

Fried, C., 1968. Privacy. Yale Law J. 77, 475–493.

Goodman, M., 2016. Future Crimes: Inside the Digital Underground and the Battle for Our Connected World. Anchor Books, New York.

Greengard, S., 2015. The Internet of Things. MIT Press, Cambridge and London.

Gubbi, J., Buyya, R., Marusic, S., et al., 2013. Internet of Things (IoT): A vision, architectural elements, and future directions. Future Gener. Comput. Syst. 29 (7), 1645–1660.

Haggerty, K., Ericson, R., 2000. The surveillant assemblage. Br. J. Sociol. 51 (4), 605–622.

Harari, Y.N., 2018. 21 Lessons for the 21st Century. Jonathan Cape, London.

Haraway, D.J., Wolfe, C., 2016. Manifestly Haraway. University of Minnesota Press, Minneapolis, United States.

Hossain, B., 2020. Critical analysis of blockchain for Internet of Everything. In: Ahmed, M., Bakrat Ullah, A., Khan Pathan, A.-S. (Eds.), Security Analytics for the Internet of Everything. CRC Press, Bocca Ratton, London, New York.

Howard, P., 2015. Pax Technica: How the Internet of Things May Set Us Free or Lock Us Up. Yale University Press, New Heaven and London.

International Telecommunications Union, 2005. ITU Internet reports: The Internet of Things. Geneva. https://www.itu.int/pub/S-POL-IR.IT-2005 (accessed 02.06.2020).

Ives, S., 2015. IoT and drones to drive wireless video surveillance. Secur. Syst. N. 18 (11), 1–2.

Johnston R., 2020. Sidewalk Labs to next venture, says former consultant. Available from: https://statescoop.com/ann-cavoukian-waterfront-toronto-digital-privacy-concerns-sidewalk-labs/ (accessed 3.09.2020).

Joy, B., 2019. Why the future doesn't need us. In: Yampolskiy, R. (Ed.),

Artificial Intelligence Safety and Security. CRC Press, Boca Raton, London, New York.

Kearns I., 2018. Crime and the pros and cons of the internet of things. Available from: http://www.police-foundation.org.uk/2018/10/crime-and-the-pros-and-cons-of-the-internet-of-things/ (accessed 03.12.2019).

Koslowski R., 2004. New technologies of border control in an Enlarged Europe. Available from: https://www.wilsoncenter.org/publication/299-new-technologies-border-control-enlarged-europe (accessed 11.09.2020).

Lee, H.J., 2015. A study on social issue solutions using the "Internet of Things" (focusing on a crime prevention camera system). Int. J. Distrib. Sens. Netw. 11 (9), 747593.

Li, S., 2017. Introduction: Securing the Internet of Things. In: Li, S., Xu, L.D. (Eds.), Securing the Internet of Things. Elsevier, New York, pp. 1–23.

Lianos, M., 2003. Social Control after Foucault. Surveill. Soc. 1 (3), 412–430.

Lyon, D., 2007. Surveillance Studies. Polity, Cambridge.

Lyon, D., 2018. The Culture of Surveillance. Polity, Cambridge.

Lyon, D., Haggerty, K., Ball, K., 2012. Introducing surveillance studies. In: Ball, K., Haggerty, K., Lyon, D. (Eds.), Routledge Handbook of Surveillance Studies. Routledge, London and New York, pp. 1–12.

McGuire, M., 2012. Technology, Crime and Justice: The Question Concerning Technomia. Routledge, London and New York.

Means Coleman, R.R., Brunton, D.-W., 2016. "You might not know her, but you know her brother": Surveillance Technology, Respectability Policing, and the Murder of Janese Talton Jackson. Souls 18 (2-4), 408–420.

Milivojevic, S., 2013. Borders, technology and mobility: Cyber-fortress Europe and its emerging Southeast frontier. Aust. J. Hum. Rights 19 (3), 99–120.

Milivojevic, S., 2019a. Border Policing and Security Technologies. Routledge, London and New York.

Milivojevic, S., 2019b. 'Stealing the fire', 2.0 style?: Technology, the pursuit for mobility, social memory and de-securitization of migration. Theor. Criminol. 23 (2), 211–227.

Milivojevic, S., Radulski, E.M., 2020. The 'future Internet' and crime: Towards a criminology of the Internet of Things. Curr. Issues Crim. Justice 32 (2), 193–207.

Muller, B., 2010. Security, Risk and Biometric State. Routledge, New York.

Neal, A., 2009. Securitization and risk at the EU border: the origins of FRONTEX. J. Common. Mark. Stud. 47 (2), 333–356.

Orr, D., Sanchez, L., 2018. Alexa, did you get that? Determining the evidentiary value of data stored by the Amazon® Echo. Digit. Invest. 24, 72–78.

Palmer D., 2018. An Internet of Things 'crime harvest' is coming unless security problems are fixed. Available from: https://www.zdnet.com/article/an-internet-of-things-crime-harvest-is-coming-unless-security-problems-are-fixed/ (accessed 20.05.2020).

Perry, S., Roda, C., 2016. Human Rights and Digital Technology: Digital Tightrope. Palgrave Macmillan Limited, London, United Kingdom.

Popescu, G., 2015. Controlling mobility: Embodying borders. In: Szary, A.-L.A., Giraut, F. (Eds.), Borderities and the Politics of Contemporary Mobile Borders. Palgrave, Baskingstoke and New York, pp. 100–115.

Roman, R., Najera, P., Lopez, J., 2011. Securing the Internet of Things. Computer 44 (9), 51–58.

TEDx Talks, 2018. IoT and Machine Learning - Changing the Future Dr Dennis Ong. 10 April 2018 https://www.youtube.com/watch?v=mlE03Fj02T09s.

Thrift, N., 2004. Remembering the technological unconscious by foregrounding knowledges of position. Environ. Plan. D: Soc. Space 22 (1), 175–190.

Thrift, N., 2005. Knowing Capitalism. Sage, London.

Tuptuk, N., Hailes, S., 2019. Crime in the age of the Internet of Things. In: Wortley, R., Sidebottom, A., Tilley, N. et al. (Eds.), Routledge Handbook of Crime Science. Routledge, London and New York.

Tvede, L., 2020. Supertrends: 50 Things You Need to Know about the Future. John Wiley & Sons, Incorporated, Newark.

Tzezana, R., 2016. Scenarios for crime and terrorist attacks using the Internet of Things. Eur. J. Futures Res. 4 (1), 18.

Vaughan-Williams, N., 2010. The UK Border Security Continuum: Virtual Biopolitics and the Simulation of the Sovereign Ban. Environ. Plan. D: Soc. Space 28 (6), 1071–1083.

Vos, M., 2018. Organizational implementation and management challenges in the Internet of Things. In: Hassan, Q., Khan, R., Madani, S. (Eds.), Internet of Things: Challenges, Advances, Applications. London and New York CRC Press, Boca Ratton, pp. 33–50.

Weber, V., 2017. The Synergetic Smart City Framework - From Idea to Reality. Estate Issues, 75–81.

Williams, J., 2016. Privacy in the age of the Internet of Things. Hum. Rights 41 (4), 14–22.

Wood, M.A., 2016. Antisocial media and algorithmic deviancy amplification: Analysing the id of Facebook's technological unconscious. Theor. Criminol. 21 (2), 168–185.

Zanella, A., Bui, N., Castellani, A., et al., 2014. Internet of Things for Smart Cities. IEEE Internet Things J. 1 (1), 22–32.

Zimmer, A., 2017. Boots on The Ground, Eyes in The Sky. (cover story). Law Enforc. Technol. 44 (9), 20–26.

5

AUTONOMOUS MOBILE ROBOTS

Kinetic machines in charge?

Introduction

Artificial intelligence and the Internet of things are the foundation for another type of emerging technology that embodies the movement and action-taking by ground, underwater, and aerial vehicles without a person on board. Welcome to the exciting new world of automation and mobile robotics, where the connection between algorithm-run smart machines and people is increasingly elusive. Until recently, we mostly used robots to automate the production in manufacturing and agriculture (industrial robots). Today, mobile robotics is one of the fastest-growing fields of scientific research (Rubio et al., 2019). Contemporary robots include a range of physically embodied machines that can perform tasks and sense and manipulate their environment with a high degree of independence. There are many types of robots: consumer robots that assist us with daily tasks (such as Roomba vacuum cleaner), education robots (an interactive PEPPER robot), entertainment robots (Furby, a robot toy that was a must-have item for children in the 2000s), humanoid robots (Sophia, the United Nation Development Programme first-ever Innovation Champion, or Atlas, a Boston Robotics humanoid robot that can develop the speed of 1.5 m/s), industrial robots (robotic arms designed to perform repetitive tasks), mobile robots (self-driving forklifts and cars, drones), social robots (a therapeutic robot Paro the seal), and others. In terms of self-sufficiency, there are teleoperated robots where a human supervisor provides some or most of the instructions (for example, rovers on Mars or robot surgeons), and autonomous robots with limited or no supervision (such as Roomba – for more info on types of robots see Cook and Zhang, 2020). This chapter focuses on two types of autonomous mobile robots: autonomous vehicles (automated self-driving or driverless cars—AVs) and unmanned aerial vehicles (UAVs; drones). The rationale to include these two types of mobile robots is their current and predicted usage, as well as likely significance for offending and crime control.

While in use for several decades, forecasts about the prevalence of mobile robots by the year 2020 were off the mark. Projections that people are going to become 'permanent backseat drivers', and that '10 million self-driving cars will be on the road by 2020' (Piper, 2020) proved to be widely inaccurate. I live in Central London and am yet to see a car without a driver trotting along Piccadilly. Similarly, claims that by 2020, drones will be used for delivery of goods in major cities in the US and the UK have not materialised. There is no doubt, however, that technology is on the rise, as is its autonomy. From initial successes such as the 2004 Defence Advanced Research Project Agency's (DARPA) *Grand Challenges,* a competition to develop driverless cars that can navigate obstacles and complete the course set in the Mojave Desert[1], the level of automation of smart machines is rising. Today, AVs and UAVs are either on Level 3 or 4 of automation. As such, they can operate autonomously in some situations with human oversight (Level 3), or are autonomous in most situations, with a pilot/driver that can take control but does not have to do so (Level 4). Like debates around AGI, there is no agreement among developers and experts regarding the timeline for level 5 automation (a complete autonomy in all conditions). Yet, increased autonomy of smart machines is bound to have an impact on individuals and communities in smart cities. Moreover, with the speed of technological expansions, many ethical and legal issues attached to this technology and its effect on offending, crime prevention, and criminal justice system of the future warrant our attention.

Experts and social commentators suggest that innovations in robotics such as full automation should go hand in hand with the humanisation of society (Bradley, 2017), calling for clear ground rules for developers and the industry more broadly. The *Three Laws of Robotics* (known as *Asimov's Law*) set by an American science fiction writer and academic Isaac Asimov in 1942 stipulate that robots:

1.   May not injure humans or, through inaction, allow a human being to come to harm;

2. Must obey orders given by humans, except where such orders might conflict with the First Law; and
3. Must protect its own existence as long as such protection does not conflict with the First or the Second Law (cited in Bradley, 2017).

While occasionally scrutinised and altered by a new generation of scientists, these rules still guide advancements in modern robotics (Bhaumik, 2018). I come to this point later in the chapter. Sustaining this development are efforts to make AI that enables autonomous robots to *learn, adopt,* and *retain* our goals (Tegmark, 2017). Humans, thus, need to be clear about what we want, articulate and ensure AI understands, adopts and retains these goals, notwithstanding its increasing autonomy. Clarity is critical, having in mind that robots powered by AI will be making value-based, moral decisions, with little or no human input. Driverless cars and drones will hypothetically be accountable for harming people as they have the potential to be—and indeed are—used against humans. While the issue of criminal liability is of importance here, this topic was explored at length in Chapter 3. The analysis presented in that chapter can be, to a great extent, applied to AVs and UAVs (for more information on the debate around criminal liability and self-driving autonomous cars, see Douma and Palodichuk, 2012; Gurney, 2015). Issues vis-à-vis privacy and surveillance will also not be re-examined as they too were covered in previous chapters. The focus of this chapter is the origins, types and expansion of autonomous vehicles and drones, followed by ethical debates around mobile robots, their potential use in offending and policing, and finally, their impact on human mobility. As with other chapters in this volume, the selection of themes covered is not exhaustive; rather, it reflects the current and predicted applications of the technology in the immediate future.

The origins, types, and advances of mobile robots

Like many other technological advancements, drones and AVs have its origins in science fiction[2]. While dating back to the 1920s (Wilson, 2012; Bagloee et al., 2016), the evolution of both technologies is linked to the rise of the military-industrial complex in the twentieth century (Barry, 2013). Indeed, as mentioned in the introduction, it was the US Department of Defence's DARPA project that led to the expansion of mobile robots. The initial military use of drones was for surveillance purposes in the Gulf War (1990–1991), in former Yugoslavia (1991–1995) and the 1999 NATO bombing of Serbia (Finn and Wright, 2012; Hayes et al., 2014). I still recall looking up the night sky with my parents in Serbia's northern province of Vojvodina, trying to decipher whether a slow-moving object above our heads was a fighter plane or, marginally less frightening, a drone that did not carry weapons. Today, UAVs are frequently used in war zones and conflict areas for surveillance and physical elimination of terror suspects and 'enemy combatants'. This application raises questions around the acceptability of drones' deployment, given Asimov's law and notion that robot ethics aims to prevent machines from harming humans (Asaro, 2006). While the overarching narrative for the use of drones in the military context is that this technology 'does the right thing with minimum collateral damage', critics have been fast to point out that the use of drones, especially drone strikes, are inhumane, pre-emptive, and amount to war crimes (Coeckelbergh, 2013; Chamayou, 2015; Wall, 2016). Other issues include targeting non-civilian and civilian populations, proportionality, just or unjust use of force, and *ius in bello* (see Enemark, 2013). As these complex issues require a thorough analysis and attention, this chapter will mostly focus on civil drones; military drones will be discussed sporadically, leaving the discussion around issues identified above for future publications.

Contemporary civil drones are used for commercial, state, recreational, community, rescue and other commercial and entertainment purposes (Finn and Wright, 2012; Boucher, 2016). Border control has been one of the key areas for the deployment of civil drones. The US border agency Customs and Border Protection signalled its interest in drones in the late 1990s, while first drones patrolled the US-Mexico border in 2003 (Barry, 2013). The expansion of driverless cars, on the other hand, has been underpinned by a road safety narrative as predictions suggested they could eliminate at least 90% of civilian road deaths (Tegmark, 2017: Chapter 3, section AI for transportation). At present, there are two types of autonomous cars that can perform driving functions without human interference or control; they are self-contained autonomous vehicles and interconnected autonomous vehicles. Self-contained vehicles rely solely on the information gathered from and within a vehicle. On the other hand, interconnected vehicles receive data from a vehicle and the outside environment, mostly through a wireless connection (Gurney, 2015). Both self-contained and interconnected vehicles have been perceived as a solution for a range of social issues, such as safer and a lower cost of transport, drink driving, and transportation for the elderly, people with limited mobility, and underage populations (Gurney, 2015; Bagloee et al., 2016; Woods, 2019). Importantly, both types of autonomous mobile robots discussed in this chapter are likely to have a significant impact on offending and crime control.

Scanning and scenario writing: Smart machines' takeover?

Since they were first spotted on the roads and in the sky, expansion of teleoperated and autonomous mobile robots generated public interest and raised questions about the nature and application of the technology. Similar to contexts around AI and the IoT, ethics in robotics as questions how should humans design, deploy, and treat robots is often the starting point when debating growth and future impact of UAVs and AVs. As broader questions around ethics and the Model of Care approach in developing AI were explored at length in Chapter 3, this chapter furthers the debate by examining additional themes relevant for mobile robotics. Contrary to the code and smart devices, the physical embodiment of mobile robots and their ability to carry and deploy weapons underpin the discussion around smart machines. They can not only 'intentionally' kill us; smart machines can and do make decisions on who to save, while their inaction can also cause injury or the death of a human. Asimov's Law and the Model of Care, thus, might fall short as experts and developers struggle to provide precise guidelines for scenarios that are often difficult to imagine (see Walsh, 2017).

On the morality of robots

The integration of AI into mobile machines and their increased level of autonomy elevates the issue of ethics as robots have the potential to, accidentally or not, cause harm. The central question is: what ethical principles, if any, should be driving the development of autonomous mobile robots? Should we consider smart machines our companion species and work to improve human-machine alliances, or should we consider them 'inferiors' and treat robots as we would like to be treated by our superiors (Walsh, 2017)? In 2010, the Engineering and Physical Science Research Council, the chief UK government body that funds and oversees AI research, developed the following basic principles for robotics:

1. Robots are multi-use tools. Robots should not be designed solely or primarily to kill or harm humans, except in the interest of national security;

2. Humans, not robots, are responsible agents. Robots should be designed; operated as far as is practicable to comply with existing laws and fundamental rights and freedoms, including privacy;
3. Robots are products. They should be designed using processes which assure their safety and security;
4. Robots are manufactured artefacts. They should not be designed in a deceptive way to exploit vulnerable users; instead, their machine nature should be transparent; and
5. The person with legal responsibility for a robot should be attributed (cited in Walsh, 2017).

We can identify several worrying trends in this 'update' of Asimov's Laws by the key governing body of one of the leading nations in AI research. The first concern is the explicit recognition that robots *can* be developed solely or primarily to kill or harm humans if the interest of national security justifies such development. There is a plethora of literature in criminology and social sciences that warns about a loosely defined national security logic, and concessions made in that regard that violate fundamental human rights and civil liberties (see works of Peter Andreas, Jennifer Chachón, Jude McCulloch, Sharon Pickering, Lucia Zedner, Dean Wilson, and others). The second worrying trend is a complete removal of agency when it comes to smart machines. While 'machine nature' is recognised to some extent in the guidelines, there is no helpful suggestions on how to preserve privacy or ensure safety, security, and transparency of robots. Finally, accountability for robots' actions is firmly located with humans, while it is not specified who should be responsible: end-users, developers, or someone else.

Experts such as Peter Asaro, Toby Walsh, and others suggest that we need a somewhat different approach when it comes to robot ethics. Asaro outlines the following three pillars of 'ethics in robotics':

- The ethical systems built into robots;
- The ethics of people who design and use robots; and
- The ethics of people who treat robots.

Ultimately, however, we should be thinking about the prospect of robots as autonomous moral agents (Asaro, 2006; see also Walsh, 2017). The narrative of a benevolent technology that focuses on harm prevention and reduction, as well as improvement of human lives and equality, is a logical extension of this discourse. Autonomous vehicles and drones are heralded as potential game-changers and technology worth investing in for the benefit of humankind. If we 'embed' the right ethics into mobile robots and ensure humans who design and use smart machines also behave ethically, the future will be much brighter.

Scientists, however, disagree on the exact approach on how to deliver the above goal: through preference, equality, or neutrality. The first approach suggests that smart machines should have a preference or ethical standards that would differentiate who lives and who does not if such situation arises. The second school of thought believes that autonomous machines should not have any preference when deciding whom to save. The third group of scholars argues that smart machines do not have the capacity to do any of this. The first approach is epitomised in the 'Moral Machine Experiment'. This online experimental platform gathered 39.6 million participants from 233 countries and territories, providing answers on moral dilemmas pertinent to the use of autonomous vehicles (Awad et al., 2018). One of the scenarios presented was a variation of the famous 'trolley problem' where you have the power to pull a lever and divert a runaway railway car. However, there are consequences for your actions: either you kill five people on the main track by not pulling a lever, or you pull it and kill one person to a siding. In the Moral Machine Experiment, an autonomous vehicle was about to crash and cannot find the trajectory that would save everyone involved. Should it be programmed to save three elderly people on a pedestrian crossing or a couple with a child in a car? The experiment found that, in general, people opt to save human lives over animals, more lives over fewer lives, and young lives over old lives (Awad et al., 2018). Studies have also found that most people would pull the lever as a response to the original trolley problem, but would choose to save themselves and would not like the car to make a decision on their behalf if this would result in their death as a passenger (Millar, 2017).

The second group of studies, however, found that people primarily want a no-preference equal treatment by the machines (Bigman and Gray, 2020). Bigman and Gray (2020) conclude that, while it might be impossible for smart machines to have a deep sense of egalitarianism, it is plausible to program them to disregard age, gender, race, and class. Therefore, we should not provide strict instructions to autonomous machines, but simply 'tell' them to do what we would and have the best interest of humans and other life forms at heart (Chase, 2018). Lastly, Harari (2018: 56–61) suggests that algorithms, however 'smart' they might be, do not understand ethics, and as such, we should not embed ethics into smart machines. Businesses and software developers adopt one of the above models when developing AVs, often with controversy. Recently, a German car giant Mercedes announced that its cars would be prioritising passengers rather than non-occupants when making the 'trolley' decisions. The German Ministry of Transportation quickly intervened, calling the practice illegal (Renda, 2018).

The development of UAVs further fuelled the debate around the moral dimension of technology. The juxtaposed notions of 'good' vs. 'bad' drone has been increasingly explored in a range of disciplines, especially the STS (Sandvik and Jumbert, 2016). The good (civil) drone is deployed to rescue, assist, save lives, and prevent adversity and crime, while the bad (military) drone is the one that kills. Yet, the line between the two is blurry. The physical distance created by using UAVs generates a moral distance as well, not just in the context of war and armed conflict. The remoteness of drone teleoperator makes it easier to eliminate the target (Coeckelbergh, 2013; Chamayou, 2015). Nevertheless, remoteness, as it will be discussed later in the chapter, can also make it easier to immobilise and endanger, even when the purported use of the technology is to help and rescue. Where the ethics debate is heading is a vital matter for criminologists, as autonomous mobile robots might commit crimes in the future, with no human input. We should monitor this space and offer our expertise on how to minimise the adverse effect of robots on crime and offending in the future Internet.

Moving robots: Killing machines on the loose?

In 2018, a self-driving Uber car operating in autonomous mode killed Elaine Herzberg, a 49-year-old woman living in Tempe, Arizona. The panic in the media was palpable, although commentators were quick to point out that human drivers kill many humans in traffic accidents every single day (Piper, 2020). Elaine Herzberg's death was compared to the death of Bridget Driscoll, the first pedestrian to ever be killed by a car in the United Kingdom in 1896 (Kunkle, 2018). For a while, Uber suspended testing of self-driving vehicles in Arizona. The questions everyone seems to be asking were: How could this happen? Is the technology ready? Drones, on the other hand, already have a reputation as 'killer robots', given their military application. As Hayes et al. (2014: 8) point out, '[f]ew technologies have captured the media's attention like drones'. Perceived as the ultimate smart weapons, drones in the military context provide an advantage in information warfare; however, they are increasingly seen as 'automated surveillance-military killing machines' (Wilson, 2012: 274). We are now used to media reports about drone attacks like the one on general Qasem Soleimani, a top commander of the Iranian Army killed in Iraq in January 2020. Drones have caused thousands of military and civilian casualties in Pakistan, Syria, Afghanistan, Yemen, and Somalia (Wall and Monahan, 2011; Hayes et al., 2014).

The use of robots—in particular, drones in war—has been extensively scrutinised in media and academia (Wall and Monahan, 2011; Coeckelbergh, 2013; Chamayou, 2015; Wall, 2016). The predominant narrative around both military and civil drones is one of a hunt, with a mixture of sci-fi and Greek and Roman mythological names used to baptise the latest machines (Milivojevic, 2016). A superior, technology-powered enforcers from the sky, thus, 'hunt and kill' the adversary fighters and prospective terrorists or identify and immobilise illegalised border crossers. From the safe space, targets in hostile areas are monitored and eliminated, by chance or design (see Chamayou, 2015). The outcome is a 'drone stare'—surveillance 'that abstract people from contexts, thereby reducing variation, difference, and noise that may impede action or introduce moral ambiguity' (Wall and Monahan, 2011: 239). Via drone use, people are reduced to targets, dead bodies to numbers, and civilian victims to collateral damage and 'bug splats' (Danchev, 2016).

Civil mobile robots tend to avoid such scrutiny. Still, as Leetaru (2019) notes, '[a]s we look into the future of driverless cars and autonomous delivery drones, one of the most existential questions of their future is how to prevent them from being used for harm'. In the future, AVs and drones will mostly be connected to one another and the infrastructure, via smart devices and sensors they carry. They will be prone to hacking and misuse and might break the law empowered by surveillance, commiting crimes such as stalking, family violence, child abuse, assault, drug trafficking, or terrorism (Boucher, 2016; Goodman, 2016). How is law enforcement to respond to these anxieties is discussed below.

Policing in the era of mobile robots

What happens when police encounter a 'criminal' mobile robot? How are police, for example, to stop autonomous vehicles? For many of us, the typical way to interact with the police is via traffic stops (Kerr, 2017; Woods, 2019). But, when we are passengers in a self-driving car that obeys traffic rules, there might be no need for such interventions. This scenario is particularly important for communities disproportionately targeted by discretionary policing practices (Joh, 2019). Fewer stops by police will certainly be beneficial for police officers as well, as it will lead to a de-escalation of risk associated with this type of police work. As Woods (2019) suggests, AVs will obey rules, making traffic stops less likely, decrease assaults against officers, and lead to an overhaul of drink-driving and licensing laws and policies. Data transmitted to and from autonomous vehicles are likely to assist in investigations of traffic incidents when they occur. Some manufacturers have been developing systems that will communicate traffic violations directly to police, by-passing humans passengers (Joh, 2019). Developers have also been testing the tools to remotely immobilise self-driving cars from an emergency hotline. Just imagine the following scenario: your self-driving car is stolen. You quickly contact the police, and they request permission to take over the vehicle. They drive the vehicle to the police station, with thieves still inside (Joh, 2019). This 'remote control' policing could undoubtedly reduce the risk associated with high-speed car chases and arrests, both for officers involved and the passengers. Indeed, many police shootings happen during stop and search attempts or car chases by police (Joh, 2019).

Emergency services use teleoperated robots such as 'public order drones' (Hayes et al., 2014; Sandvik, 2016) or bomb defusing mobile robots for a range of purposes, such as surveillance, public order, safe-guarding persons and objects, and preventing or detecting crime (Finn and Wright, 2012; Marin, 2016). A robot that was sent to a house to taser an armed offender under the direction of the supervisor prompted a debate on using robots to save lives (Cook and Zhang, 2020). Some researchers suggests that public acceptance of police drones is high (Boucher, 2016). Given that mobile robots and other technological advancements used by law enforcement integrate AI and the IoT technology, future policing is likely to be big data analysis and intervention, rather than hands-on police approach (Kerr, 2017; Renda, 2018). Although 'weaponised civil drones' may or may not patrol our skies and roads in the future (for more context see Finn and Wright, 2012; Sandvik, 2016; Marin, 2016), policing will certainly change. It may well be offshored to businesses, agencies, universities, banks, and citizens. Rather than providing officers on the ground, customers will need to purchase the technology, affiliated (or not) with the local police department. One such example is an outdoor security robot K5. The machine that visually resembles Star Wars' much-loved smart robot R2-D2 is deployed to patrol the streets, university campuses, parking lots, sports stadiums, hospitals, and other public spaces in the US (Markman, 2018). As the company claims on its website, the future is already here. Powered by AI, K5 promises to stop the crime before it happens, while wearing the official police logo, or acting as an independent 'security guard'.

Like discussions vis-à-vis the IoT and AI, it is dubious whether the advances of mobile robots will eradicate the danger of over-policing, discretionary policing practices, and pre-crime. The narrative of benevolent technology should be taken with caution: even if/when technology becomes fully autonomous, the question of foundational algorithms and limitations of machine learning remain. A vast amount of data collected and transmitted by mobile robots could be a vital investigative tool for law enforcement, as discussed in Chapter 4. However, they could, like scenarios investigated in previous chapters, lead to pre-crime. Moreover, growth and further developments in autonomous mobile robotics are a concern for crime control agencies. To date, drones have been used for stalking, intimidation of police officers and citizens, drug smuggling (especially to prisons), spying on homes and looking for potential targets for burglaries (Rogers, 2019). In the future, this list is likely to get longer. In December 2019, police struggled to disable drones that interrupted air traffic at Gatwick airport in the UK. For three days, over 29 drone sightings caused a significant disruption in air travel just before Christmas (Rogers, 2019). With more drones used for commercial purposes and deliveries, police intervention might be necessary more often[3]. The question we need to ask is how will the police engage with disorderly and criminal behaviour of mobile robots and what will the impact of such interventions be, especially on vulnerable and marginalised social groups (Finn and Wright, 2012). We need to be wary of the 'mission creep' that might see the increase in police use of autonomous mobile robots for other purposes.

Swarms of drones powered by AI that communicate with one another are already a reality. Soon, drones that work as a team will make informed, and to some extent, autonomous decisions based on data they collect or receive from each other, the environment, and human instructors. They will have autonomy in reaching set goals and might create new goals. We need to be prepared for the scenario that some drones or AVs in a swarm, for example, might distract the attention of police while others from the pack offend. We have seen an example of this in the 2019 attack on Saudi oil fields, where several drones acted as a decoy while others committed an attack that was a significant blow to the Saudi economy, but also their US protectors (Rogers, 2019). Will police resort to hacking or other denial of service interventions to counter crimes committed by or via autonomous mobile robots? Critically, what new police powers will unfold, promoted as necessary to combat a new threat?

Enforcing immobility: 'Dronisation' of 'roborders'

Border security and regulating mobility have been at the forefront of state intervention for over three decades. Apparent failure in traditional border control measures prompted the quest for 'more sophisticated, flexible, and mobile devices of tracking, filtration, and exclusion' (Vukov and Sheller, 2013: 225). Separating kinetic elites from kinetic underclass has been fortified through series of interventions in border management that include technological advancements deployed at the border and beyond (Neal, 2009; Milivojevic, 2013; Wilson, 2014; Sandvik, 2016; Milivojevic, 2019). Given the importance of border control in the political and social context, it is hardly surprising that the issue of finding a technological 'solution' for the illegalised mobility 'problem' emerged as a holy grail of contemporary politics.

Transpiring digital technologies such as mobile robots are the new frontier in this quest, both as part of the problem and a potential solution for issues at hand. Recently, the FBI warned that driverless cars are likely to be used for human smuggling, drug and sex trafficking (Cowper and Levin, 2019). At the same time, the use of drones by organised crime and drug gangs has been identified as a concern in some countries (see, for example, Custers, 2016). Using technology for offending, however, is overshadowed by its potential use for cross-border crime prevention and regulating mobility more broadly. Surveillance from the sky has emerged as a preferred method in strengthening risky borderlands, as drones have been increasingly deployed to identify and immobilise populations from the Global South. As Csernatoni (2018) suggests, we are witnessing 'dronisation' of borders, the process of developing and implementing high-tech securitised border control policies across the Global North, under an umbrella of combatting crime. Drones have been transferred 'from the global battlespace to the humanitarian emergency zone' (Sandvik and cLohne, 2014: 145).

The notion of 'drones for human rights' and a 'humanitarian drone' that could prevent, if not eliminate human suffering inflicted by smugglers, traffickers, and transnational criminal networks underpin the development of drones in border policing (Sandvik and Lohne, 2014; Sandvik, 2016;

Jumbert, 2016). Not only could drones rescue innocent victims; they are seen as critical tools for preventing deaths at risky borderlands. There is an important caveat here, prompted by the question who operates the drone and for what purpose. As Koslowski and Schulzke (2018) suggest, drones operated by NGOs and rescue agencies—but also the state—can and do save lives. Their use is a mixture of costs and benefits, and the best way forward is to maximise the later and minimise the former. The concern identified by scholars and social commentators (Hayes et al., 2014; Milivojevic, 2016; Marin, 2016), however, is that the narrative of a humanitarian drone, especially in the context of patrolling the Mediterranean, has been used to conceal the main aim of their deployment. The supposed search and rescue element of drone surveillance obscures the realities of increased surveillance of mobile populations, especially illegalised non-citizens, with the overarching goal of disrupting their mobility projects. One study analysing the use drones in border surveillance suggests that technology has mostly been used to gather information about movements of illegalised non-citizens in countries of origin or transit, not their rescue (Marin, 2016). Yet, invisible 'eyes in the sky' in border policing remain largely unchallenged and desired (Boucher, 2016). The decision on who is in and who is out, who can cross and who is to be immobilised is, while still in the hands of humans, increasingly based on data captured, processed, and analysed by a range of non-human technological advancements.

The impact of surveillance-based, drone-led border policing on mobile bodies caught in the drone stare is further dehumanisation of men, women, and children on the move. By creating 'mechanical distance' (Grossman, cited in Sandvik and Lohne, 2014) between non-human (drone) and human (guards and border crossers), people are reduced to targets, numbers, collateral damage, transferees, lawbreakers, or illegals that need to be detected, immobilised, and removed. 'Targets' look like ants and germs—objects that need to be controlled, scrutinised, surveyed and, if necessary, immobilised (Wall and Monahan, 2011; Milivojevic, 2016). As we reduce bodies to red dots on the thermal imaging screen, previously mentioned notion of border policing as a 'hunt' comes to the fore (Milivojevic, 2019). The desired outcome is the removal of threat and the restoration of order at the border and beyond. Forced immobility is achieved primarily in countries of origin and transit for illegalised migrants, prior to reaching the physical borders of the Global North. Notably, a human cost—so clearly visible in the context of military drones—is almost absent here, hidden behind the smokescreen of search and rescue (Milivojevic, 2016).

Border policing of the future is expected to bring interconnected and increasingly autonomous UAVs and AVs likely to be deployed not just to immobilise, but to engage in pre-crime anticipation and identification of possible border violations before people embark on risky journeys. Smart machines could tap into devices border crossers carry or have embedded in their body (Campbell, 2019), and use data to ascertain—potentially on their own—whether people are a threat or not. While this synopsis might seem far-fetched, similar projects are already in preparation across the Global North.[4] 'Roborder' might be just around the corner, with mobile robots as autonomous (and potentially armed) enforcersof border regimes.

Theorising mobile robots: Companion species with life on their own?

Autonomous mobile robots are an example of distancing technologies. Driverless cars and UAVs are inventions that, at the core, embed a growing absence of humans in their operational activities, as well as the depletion of the human-thing alliance. Robots are increasingly independent of their human counterparts and rely on machine learning and information via the IoT/AI-powered networks to achieve set or generate new goals. Human and non-human actors in these networks are becoming dissociated from one another, while the links between non-humans continue to grow. Understanding this process is essential for our comprehension and engagement with future crimes linked to mobile robots, given their potential to almost instantly endanger and harm many people.

The absence of a human body in, or human engagement with mobile robots translates into a moral dilemma that is intrinsically linked to the human body. We want to make sure that when it comes to decision making, as we get removed from the decision process, some safeguards are put in place. We also want to make sure that technology will continue to obey Asimov's Laws—or whatever 'update' experts and the scientific community agree upon. Reducing mobile robots to inferior species, however, is not the trajectory I would advocate for, particularly given some worrying trends in the ethics in robotics identified above. While I am not engaging in a debate around 'robot abuse',[4] this is an important question to ponder. Currently, mobile robots are defined by a critical juxtaposition: they eliminate and bypass distance, yet they create more distance between humans and technology. Driverless cars and drones enable connection and mobility, yet they increasingly limit it. They were supposed to reduce violence and harm, yet they produce it. In the critical literature on the use of drones in military and non-military contexts authors such as Neocleous, Singh, Kelly and Prasad suggest that aerial violence legitimised in the military context easily transfers to the local, aiding the fight against the poor, marginalised and socially excluded (Wall, 2016). The use of mobile robots, as demonstrated in this chapter, can result in practices that enhance social exclusion, if not physical elimination of a range of target groups, such as illegalised border crosses and terror suspects. Progress in mobile robotics is likely to further these conundrums, particularly given smart machines' increased autonomy.

A question that needs answering is whether the development of autonomous mobile robots such as AVs and UAVs should prompt a rethinking of crime control. As it was debated in the context of self-driving cars, the development of smart machines could potentially reduce discretionary and discriminatory practices that disproportionately target racial and ethnic minorities. This outcome might eventuate not because technology is colour-blind; it is because the development of mobile robots is likely to decrease the need for such interventions. The use of drones in policing, while clearly the extension of the militarisation of police practices, can also lead to the reduction of discriminatory policing practices as surveillance from above will target everyone. Yet, while the development of mobile robots might result in lessening instances of discrimination when it comes to enforcing law and order, we cannot know on which side the coin will fall, and whether the expansion of autonomous smart machines will, in fact, result in further violations of human rights and civil liberties of risky and marginalised populations.

While in this chapter I intentionally did not focus on the capacity of autonomous mobile robots to gather, collect, transmit, and exchange data about us, our daily habits, and movements, this is a concern. Whether on the road, in our houses, workplaces, or public spaces, information about us will be stored, exchanged, and analysed. A belief that technology is ultimately a driver for good underpins the development of autonomous vehicles and drones. Technology, thus, can save lives (even in the context of military 'killer drones' as targeted killings supposedly reduce the number of collateral casualties), assist in arresting offenders, prevent unauthorised entry to the territory of nation-states, and even pre-empt crimes. This narrative builds on the notion that security technologies could protect borders and the nation, and regain control over mobility mostly in countries of origin and transit (Jumbert, 2016; Milivojevic, 2019), but also in countries of destination. The idea of technology as a helper in restoring the order at the border and beyond is likely to gain more traction in the coming years.

Contrary to the development of the IoT, mobile robots' advancements will not result in the technological unconscious. The notion that technology will lead to a better quality of life and improved regulatory mechanisms that will aid the state in upholding public order, regulating mobility, and preventing or disrupting criminal activity underpins the industry. Questioning it will be labelled as disruptive: how can anyone be against technology that can save migrants drowning at sea, or reduce the number of traffic accidents? Drones and AVs are perhaps the best examples of techno-utopia where even when we know that machines have been creating, and will continue to create harm, we choose to believe in their benevolence. We believe that ultimately, smart machines will have an ethical code and when left to make their own decisions will make the right ones. But will they?

Conclusion

Mobile robots are here to stay, and yet, we seem to be 'sleepwalking into the bright future' (Walsh, 2017: Section: Ethical limits). Smart kinetic machines are increasingly self-governing, and the disconnect between humans and robots is likely to grow in decades to come. The growth of distancing technologies brings moral, legal, and societal ambiguities that need careful investigation. As Nourbakhsh (2013: xxi) suggests,

> [t]he robot future will challenge our sense of privacy. It will redefine our assumptions about human autonomy and free will. As we face more intelligent robots, so we discover new forms of identity and machine intelligence. Our moral universe will be tested by robot cruelty and robot-human relations.

These supposedly benevolent innovations are becoming super-powerful weapons in crime prevention and mobility control, but can they relieve us from the troubles created by humans, such as discrimination, immobilisation, and physical elimination? A recent shift in semantics, the argument that mobile robots can save lives, is the metaphor that lacks evidence. The 'good' mobile robots might be the hallmark of the future policing, but we need to be careful about what we wish for. Importantly, the human costs of such interventions, carefully hidden in the debate, need to be clearly outlined and analysed.

Advances in mobile robotics are intrinsically neoliberal and deliver significant profits for the companies behind it. Corporatisation and privatisation of security is nothing new in the area of criminal justice; when it comes to mobile robotics, this development certainly requires close attention. While technology can indeed yield positive results when it comes to crime-fighting and prevention, we should ask difficult questions pertinent to who benefits from it before we jump to the conclusion that smart machines work and we need to embrace them. In particular, the links between security corporations and criminal justice agencies, such as law enforcement, must be more closely scrutinised in the future. Transparency and independent evaluations are critical elements that need to accompany the development of technology and its implementation in the criminal justice setting.

Mobile robots will continue to play an essential role in detecting and immobilising the 'Other' across the borderlands and beyond. To problematise such state of affairs, the drone stare needs to be deconstructed. At the same time, broader social contexts of vulnerability, exploitation, victimisation, and human rights violation need to be positioned at the very centre of the debate. Such framing is even more critical given that people refuse, and will keep rejecting, to be 'petrified and immobilised by the drone stare' (Wall and Monahan, 2011: 250). Yet, to find our way back to the human-machine alliance, we need a joint effort by humans, and maybe a helping hand of another type of DFT explored in the next chapter.

Notes

1 With very little success at first, only to see a range of successful attempts three years later – see Davies (2018).
2 Clark reminds us that '[t]he first major twentieth century anti-utopian novel – 25 years before Orwell's 1984 – imagined drones (aeros) as the means by which the government observed and repressed the population' (p. 231). See Clark (2014).
3 Despite 'geo-fencing' parameters embedded in many civil drones that restrict where you could fly them. See https://www.dji.com/uk/flysafe/geo-map.
4 A video of developers, testers and users 'abusing' Boston Dynamic robots have been watched over 4 million times on YouTube: https://www.youtube.com/watch?v=4PaTWufUJqqI1

References

Asaro, P., 2006. What should we want from a robot ethic? Int. Rev. Inf. Ethics 6 (12/2006), 9–16.

Awad, E., Dsouza, S., Kim, R., et al., 2018. The moral machine experiment. Nature 563 (7729), 59–64.

Bagloee, S.A., Tavana, M., Asadi, M., et al., 2016. Autonomous vehicles: challenges, opportunities, and future implications for transportation policies. J. Mod. Transportation 24 (4), 284–303.

Barry, T., 2013. Drones over the homeland: expansion of scope and lag in governance. Brown J. World Aff. 19 (2), 65–80.

Bhaumik, A., 2018. Mobile Robotics: Theory and Implementation. CRC Press LLC, Boca Raton, United States.

Bigman, Y., Gray, K., 2020. Life and death decisions of autonomous vehicles. Nature 579 (7797), E1–E2.

Boucher, P., 2016. 'You Wouldn't have Your Granny Using Them': Drawing boundaries between acceptable and unacceptable applications of civil drones. Sci. Eng. Ethics 22 (5), 1391–1418.

Bradley, G., 2017. The Good ICT Society: From Theory to Actions. Routledge, London, United Kingdom.

Campbell, Z., 2019. Swarm of drones, piloted by Aritficial Intelligence, may soon patrol Europeas borders. The Intercept. 11 May 2019.

Chamayou, G., 2015. Drone Theory. Penguin Books Limited, UK.

Chase, C., 2018. Surviving AI. Three Cs, Bradford.

Clark, R., 2014. Understanding the drone epidemic. Comput. Law Soc. Rev. 30 (3), 230–246.

Coeckelbergh, M., 2013. Drones, information technology, and distance: mapping the moral epistemology of remote fighting. Ethics Inf. Technol. 15 (2), 87–98.

Cook, G., Zhang, F., 2020. Mobile Robots: Navigation, Control and Sensing, Surface Robots and AUVs. John Wiley & Sons, Incorporated, Newark, United States.

Cowper T., Levin B., 2019. Autonomous Vehicles: How Will They Challenge Law Enforcement? Available from: https://leb.fbi.gov/articles/featured-articles/autonomous-vehicles-how-will-they-challenge-law-enforcement (accessed 11.03.2020).

Csernatoni, R., 2018. Constructing the EU's high-tech borders: FRONTEX and dual-use drones for border management. Eur. Secur. 27 (2), 175–200.

Custers, B., 2016. The Future of Drone Use: Opportunities and Threats from Ethical and Legal Perspectives. T.M.C. Asser Press, The Hague, Netherlands.

Danchev, A., 2016. Bug splat: the art of the drone. Int. Aff. 92 (3), 703–713.

Davies, A., 2018. The WIRED guide to self-driving cars. Wired. https://www.wired.com/story/guide-self-driving-cars/.

Douma, F., Palodichuk, S., 2012. Criminal liability issues created by autonomous vehicles. St. Clara Law Rev. 52 (4), 1157–1169.

Enemark, C., 2013. Armed Drones and the Ethics of War: Military Virtue in a Post-Heroic Age. Routledge, London and New York.

Finn, R.L., Wright, D., 2012. Unmanned aircraft systems: surveillance, ethics and privacy in civil applications. Comput. Law Secur. Rev. 28 (2), 184–194.

Goodman, M., 2016. Future Crimes: Inside the Digital Underground and the Battle for Our Connected World. Anchor Books, New York.

Gurney, J., 2015. Driving into the unknown: examining the crossroads of criminal law and autonomous vehicles. Wake For. J. Law Policy 5 (2), 393–442.

Harari, Y.N., 2018. 21 Lessons for the 21st Century. Jonathan Cape, London.

Hayes, B., Jones, C., Toepfer, E., 2014. EURODRONES Inc. Transnational Institute and Statewatch, Amsterdam.

Joh, E., 2019. Automated seizures: police stops of self-driving cars. N. Y. Univ. Law Rev. 94, 292–314.

Jumbert, M.G., 2016. Creating the EU drone: control, sorting, and search and rescue at sea. In: Sandvik, K.B., Jumbert, M.G. (Eds.), The Good Drone. Routledge, London, United Kingdom.

Kerr, O., 2017. How self-driving cars could determine the future of policing. The Washington Post, 16 June.

Koslowski, R., Schulzke, M., 2018. Drones along borders: border security UAVs in the United States and the European Union. Int. Stud. Perspect. 19 (4), 305–324.

Kunkle, F., 2018. Fatal crash with self-driving car was a first—like Bridget Driscoll's was 121 years ago with one of the first cars. The Washington Post, 22 March.

Leetaru, K., 2019. How do we stop driverless cars and autonomous delivery drones from becoming weapons? Forbes. https://www.forbes.com/sites/kalevleetaru/201 9/08/22/how-do-we-stop-driverless-cars-and-autonomous-delivery-drones-from-becoming-weapons/#6f88dce176fa.

Marin, L., 2016. The humanitarian drone and the borders: unveiling the rationales underlying the deployment of drones in border surveillance. In: Custers, B. (Ed.), The Future of Drone Use: Opportunities and Threats from Ethical and Legal Perspectives. The Hague. T.M.C. Asser Press, Germany, pp. 115–132.

Markman, J., 2018. Security robot works at intersection of AI and Crime. Forbes, 31 October.

Milivojevic, S., 2013. Borders, technology and mobility: cyber-fortress Europe and its emerging southeast frontier. Aust. J. Hum. Rights 19 (3), 99–120.

Milivojevic, S., 2016. Re-bordering the Peripheral Global North and Global South: game of drones, immobilising mobile bodies and decentring perspectives on drones in border policing. In: Završnik, A. (Ed.), Drones and Unmanned Aerial Systems. Springer, Cham, pp. 83–100.

Milivojevic, S., 2019. Border Policing and Security Technologies. Routledge, London and New York.

Millar, J., 2017. Ethics settings for autonomous vehicles. In: Lin, P., Abney, K., Jenkins, R. (Eds.), Robot Ethics 2.0: From Autonomous Cars to Artificial Intelligence. Oxford University Press, Oxford, pp. 20–34.

Neal, A., 2009. Securitization and risk at the EU border: the origins of FRONTEX. J. Common Mark. Stud. 47 (2), 333–356.

Nourbakhsh, I.R., 2013. Robot Futures. MIT Press, Cambridge, United States.

Piper K., 2020. It's 2020. Where are our self-driving cars? Available from: https://www.vox.com/future-perfect/2020/2/14/21063487/self-driving-cars-autonomous-vehicles-waymo-cruise-uber (accessed 06.03.2020.).

Renda, A., 2018. Ethics, algorithms and self-driving cars – a CSI of the 'trolley problem'. CEPS Policy Insights, 2, 1–15.

Rogers, J., 2019. The dark side of our drone future. Bulletin of the Atomic Sciences, 4 October. https://thebulletin.org/2019/10/the-dark-side-of-our-drone-future/

Rubio, F., Valero, F., Llopis-Albert, C., 2019. A review of mobile robots: concepts, methods, theoretical framework, and applications. Int. J. Adv. Robotic Syst. 16 (2), 1729881419839596.

Sandvik, K., 2016. The political and moral economies of dual technology transfers: arming police drones. In: Završnik, A. (Ed.), Drones and Unmanned Aerial Systems: Legal and Social Implications for Security and Surveillance. Springer, Cham, Heildelberg, New York, Dordrecht, London, pp. 45–66.

Sandvik, K.B., Jumbert, M.G., 2016. The Good Drone. Routledge, London, United Kingdom.

Sandvik, K.B., Lohne, K., 2014. The rise of the humanitarian drone: giving content to an emerging concept. Millennium 43 (1), 145–164.

Tegmark, M., 2017. Life 3.0: Being Human in the Age of Artificial Intelligence. Penguin Books Limited.

Vukov, T., Sheller, M., 2013. Border work: surveillant assemblages, virtual fences, and tactical counter-media. Soc. Semiotics 23 (2), 225–241.

Wall, T., 2016. Ordinary emergency: drones, police, and geographies of legal terror. Antipode 48 (4), 1122–1139.

Wall, T., Monahan, T., 2011. Surveillance and violence from afar: the politics of drones and liminal security-scapes. Theor. Criminol. 15 (3), 239–254.

Walsh, T., 2017. It's Alive!: Artificial Intelligence from the Logic Piano to Killer Robots. La Trobe University Press, in conjunction with Black Incorporated, Melbourne.

Wilson, D., 2012. Military surveillance. In: Haggerty, K., Lyon, D. (Eds.), Routledge Handbook of Surveillance Studies. Routledge, New York, pp. 269–276.

Wilson, D., 2014. Border militarization, technology and crime control. In: Pickering, S., Ham, J. (Eds.), The Routledge Handbook on Crime and International Migration. Routledge, London and New York, pp. 141–154.

Woods, J., 2019. Autonomous vehicles and police de-escalation. Northwest. Univ. Law Rev. 114, 74–103.

6

BLOCKCHAIN

The game-changer?

Introduction

The final digital frontier technology analysed in this book is blockchain, a subset of Distributed Ledger Technology (DLT). This technology is similar yet distinctive compared to other emerging technologies. Analogous to AI, the IoT, and autonomous mobile robots, blockchain has computer algorithms at its core. As such, blockchain is ultimately a digital technology. This technology exists entirely in the digital realm and requires special tools to be seen and comprehended. However, blockchain is different from other technologies discussed in the book firstly because its current use is primarily in the financial sector. This application is not surprising given that technology was developed to support cryptocurrencies. You might not be familiar with the concept of blockchain, yet you have probably heard about bitcoin and a mysterious person(s) Satoshi Nakamoto who wrote an essay about the now-famous cryptocurrency in 2008. Bitcoin was launched in 2009 and has since changed the nature of FinTech. At the time of writing (July 2020), the value of bitcoin was around 8,400 UK pounds (in December 2017 one bitcoin was worth almost 15,000 pounds). Bitcoin marked the beginning of the rise of virtual or digital currencies. As of July 2020, there were almost 6,000 cryptocurrencies in operation worldwide (according to coinmarketcap.com). Compared to AI and the IoT blockchain is still in its infancy and the technology is not pervasive in everyday application.

While a majority of us use some form of Siri or Alexa (weak AI), smart door locks or light bulbs (the IoT), or semi-autonomous cars (autonomous mobile robots), many have never invested in or in any other way 'handled' bitcoin or other blockchain-based innovation. Some authors suggest that it will take between 10 and 20 years for this technology to become mainstream (Al-Saqaf, 2018). As a self-confessed tech geek who researches the intersection of technology and crime for almost 20 years, I admit that blockchain and cryptocurrency have been quite a mystery for me until very recently. There are other points of departure that separate blockchain from the rest of emerging technologies. While AI, mobile robots, and the IoT are almost universally hailed as innovations likely to make a significant mark in the future, the jury is still out when it comes to the future and potential utilisation of blockchain. Academics, public commentators, business people, and entrepreneurs seem divided about the prospect of blockchain-based innovations. While its financial applications are undisputable, just how much blockchain will impact other industries is anyone's guess.

After some deliberation, I decided to include blockchain in this volume, but not because of its implementation in FinTech or the potential to combat financial crimes. My motivation is its promise to drive future innovations, given blockchain's merger with the IoT and AI. Moreover, this technology could play an essential role in addressing various concerns about the application of other DFTs. Blockchain and DLT could also alter offending and victimisation, from preventing human trafficking and modern slavery, addressing vulnerabilities pertinent to security in smart homes and cities, to assisting agencies and governments in regulating migration and mobility.

While not without critics, blockchain and cryptocurrencies are acknowledged as one of the most influential innovations of the twenty-first century (Briggs et al., 2019; Chowdhury, 2019; Baucherel, 2020) that have the potential to be as disruptive and transformative as the Internet (Adams et al., 2018). Like other frontier technologies, it is difficult to ascertain just how much of the interest and noise around this technology is hype, and whether blockchain will indeed be the leading innovation of the Web (and Life) 3.0. Its application currently extends from FinTech to other industries such as trade, healthcare, politics and government affairs, and legal matters. Blockchain is poised to be an essential tool in the design of future smart cities (Baucherel, 2020; Magnuson, 2020) and in achieving Sustainable Development Goals (SDGs) as defined by the United Nations (Adams et al., 2018; Wintermeyer, 2019). As this chapter explores, the potential of blockchain is not only in its ability to bypass the central body (such as banks or government agencies) in financial and other transactions. Indeed, blockchain and bitcoin were designed to be 'radically democratic' (Magnuson, 2020; see also Danaylov, 2016: Section: Andreas Antonopoulos) and bring financial power back to the people by removing the central authority from the equation. The advances in technology have been driven by an egalitarian view of the world in which anyone with a computer could have access to digital money and exchange it without paying fees. Blockchain emerged from the cypherpunk movement[1] which sought to decentralise decision-making on the Internet and reduce governments and corporations' power by ensuring privacy and securing emails and other forms of communication through cryptography and virtual currencies (Magnuson, 2020). The power should lie with users who maintain and ensure the operations of the network by consensus. Finally, users of the technology remain anonymous, at least to some extent, preventing surveillance and oversight by the state and commercial entities.

Blockchain's prospective impact on offending, crime prevention, and the criminal justice system is significant and not limited to financial crimes. Nevertheless, there has been a little reflection in the literature on blockchains' beneficial and detrimental use, its potential to address deficiencies identified with other DFTs, and whether DLTs could bolster diminishing human-thing assemblages. This chapter will not engage in potential shortcomings of the technology, such as, for example, the fact that blockchain consensus mechanisms are usually achieved by strong computational power[2] or a previous status[3] of participants. The chapter aims to present technology and its future trajectory relevant for criminologists and social scientists, using the foresight approach; a detailed critique of the blockchain's ins and outs is best left to the scientists, FinTech, and IT experts.

Blockchaining the world

For social scientists and not-so-financially-savvy laypersons, the concept of blockchain might prove a bit difficult to understand at first. Blockchain is 'a public record of information, stored and maintained through a decentralised system of peers, and secured by sophisticated cryptographic algorithms' (Magnuson, 2020: 60). It is a record of transactions that cannot be altered or deleted (Tvede, 2020). As mentioned in the introduction, blockchain and DLT were first used in developing the cryptocurrency bitcoin in 2008. Today, this technology has been used in a range of commercial and non-commercial applications.

What makes blockchain unique is that it is a database—a record of documents, images or transactions—that are *simultaneously held* in several locations. The database, thus, is not located in one, centralised processor but in peer-to-peer (P2P) distributed networks. Data held in ledgers is small and encrypted; it is erroneous to think about blockchain as an extensive, immediately legible database (Baucherel, 2020). Every node (a member of the network) has a copy of the ledger and two keys: a public key available to everyone in the network used to confirm the identity of the sender, and a private key which is used to create a digital signature for transactions. The ledger has a growing list of records that users put in, called blocks. Each block has several key components: the block identifier, data, a timestamp of the individual entry, a cryptographic hash that prevents modification of verified data, and a link to the next block. When the new block containing information or transaction arrives, it is validated and authorised by block miners (or forgers, depending on which system of validation blockchain adopts) and added to the block. Most or all the members of the network must agree that the transaction on the block is accurately recorded (this is called *consensus mechanism*), after which point, the block is immutable. Miners receive remuneration for this service that is essential for the survival of the chain, often in forms of a local currency or cryptocurrency. The winning miner is the one who solves a complex mathematical problem first, usually with a powerful computer with high processing power; this is a very energy-intensive process. When more than 50% or all the nodes agree that the miner solved the problem correctly and verify the new block is accurate, the chain is updated. If participants disagree on the block, the block is left out of the chain (and is colloquially called a 'fork'). Forks are sometimes introduced by developers who use this technique to incite a change in the chain, for example, to introduce new rules for validating the transaction, or the new value of the cryptocurrency.

Blockchain technology, thus, has the following common features:

- It is open, verifiable, and permanent by nature;
- A decentralised consensus must be achieved to create a new block;
- Transactions are immutable; once a transaction is validated a new block is created and the previous one cannot be altered without the agreement of the majority of participants in the chain;
- It is managed in a decentralised network;
- It establishes digital trust; and
- It is secure by design (Chowdhury, 2019).

There are different types of blockchain systems, such as permissionless and permissioned blockchains. Permissionless or public blockchains are the ones everyone with a computer and the Internet access can join (i.e. one does not need permission to participate). The most well-known example of permissionless blockchain is bitcoin. As will be discussed later, this of course does not mean that a person will be successful in earning bitcoin just by having a computer and Internet access. Permissioned chains, on the other hand, are private and new actors are approved by existing participants or nodes (van Rijmenam and Ryan, 2019).

The final concept to flag at this point is so-called 'smart contracts'. As with many inventions in the realm of digital frontier technologies, the name is somewhat confusing as smart contracts are neither smart nor contracts. They are computer protocols that facilitate and verify trans actions without the third party. They operate within 'if this x, then y' module: the computer runs the program—x happens (the settlement date on your mortgage agreement) and y is automatically validated and exe-cuted (the asset goes to a buyer). Smart contracts and their importance will be explored later in the chapter.

A feature of blockchain that is critical for its applications in other industries and relevant for criminologists is blockchain's potential to 'establish the most sophisticated tracking and transparency systems that we have seen to date' (van Rijmenam and Ryan, 2019: Section 1.4: Seven Wicked Problems). This feature is particularly important in areas of social engagement where counting and tracking people, goods, or services is of essence. For example, during primary elections in two counties in West Virginia in 2018 the authorities allowed electorates to register their votes in a public blockchain. Voters were required to post a photo ID and a video of their face on an app; once their identity was verified, the app enabled their access to a public blockchain where they cast their vote and embedded it to the public blockchain. While the test went well, people were somewhat reluctant to adopt the technology. Regardless of this initial hesitation, and despite experts' concern around its usability and privacy, blockchain's use in general elections across the world is on the map (Magnuson, 2020). During the recent COVID-19 crisis, scientists in the UK suggested that blockchain could mitigate risks vis-à-vis contamination in supply chains in the post-pandemic world. They implied the technology could enable a 'Coronavirus Clearance Certificate' that could be issued to organisations, products, and maybe even people to confirm that they followed instructions and appropriate steps to minimise the risk associated with the virus. As Olinga Taeed, a visiting professor at Birmingham City University argued, '[t]he certificate confirms that a supplier adheres to highest standards of public health, sustainability, anti-bribery and even modern slavery' (cited in Hulliet, 2020). Many excellent resources explain the nature and development of blockchain and DLT if you wish to further your knowledge on this fascinating technology (Draper and Romans, 2018; Chowdhury, 2019; Baucherel, 2020; Magnuson, 2020).

Four broad groups of concerns shadow the use of blockchain. The first group contends that blockchain will not empower everyone; quite the opposite, the technology might amplify some social injustices based on gender, race, economic status, and education. The second suggests that blockchain will benefit the rich and those with resources. The third points out that, like every technology, blockchain could, and is likely to, be abused. Finally, critics worry that blockchain might simply replace one form of governance with another (for more details see Reijers and Coeckelbergh, 2018). Without going into details on this but having in mind some limitations of technology, I now turn to the overview of current and potential future relevance of blockchain to offending and crime control.

Scanning and scenario writing: The impact of blockchain and cryptocurrencies

Given that blockchain has been developed to support digital crypto-currencies, its association with crime and offending is mostly in the area of financial crime (Goodman, 2016; Houben and Snyers, 2018). However, foresight approach suggests that blockchain applications relevant for criminology are likely to be in other domains as well, such as mobility, identity, and tracking of people, goods, and services.

From 'Wild West' to 'Silk Road': Blockchain, cryptocurrencies and offending

In popular culture but also among IT professionals and coders (including my brother-in-law), cryptocurrency and blockchain users are often portrayed within the 'Wild West' narrative. In the cyberspace where morals and ethics are not upheld as essential values in digital relationships, all sorts of desperados, bullies, outlaws, and cowboys seem to roam and interact (for more, see Magnuson, 2020). Individuals and groups on the other side of the law have welcomed certain features of blockchain, such as its relative anonymity and untraceability. Cryptocurrencies have been used by organised crime since 2011 (Chowdhury, 2019), with several multi-million-dollar criminal enterprises built almost entirely on bitcoin (Burks, 2017; van Wegberg et al., 2018). The criminal activity enabled or supported by bitcoin has been found in both 'legal' bitcoin exchange markets, but also on the dark web, where technology-enabled 'traditional' crimes such as tax evasion, drug offences, extortion, money laundering, and corruption[4] lurk. A bitcoin exchange BTC has been identified an indispensable platform for such offences. Its founder, Alexander Vinnik, served as a 'one-stop-shop' for major organised crime rings, handling over US$9 bn in bitcoin transactions (Magnuson, 2020). 'Regular' users also seem to be tempted by this technology. A study done in 2018 by researchers at Sydney University estimated that 24 million bitcoin users—some 25% of all users—accounted for illicit activities (Chowdhury, 2019; Magnuson, 2020). Blockchain technology and cryptocurrencies are used to buy illegal drugs, weapons, and other illicit goods and services. This application happens on the deep web—an unindexed part of the World Wide Web, and the dark web that hosts black markets for trading these goods and services. Users remain relatively anonymous (they are pseudonymised, not anonymised) while the information about the transaction and goods and services is detailed in the chain. Dark web markets such as *Silk Road* operated exclusively on bitcoin (Chowdhury, 2019; Baucherel, 2020). The use of cryptocurrencies for the drug trade, tax evasion, corruption, money laundering, terrorism financing, and other offences prompted calls to ban certain features of digital currencies such as untraceability of users (Houben and Snyers, 2018). Anonymity in blockchain, however, is not absolute; instead, it is a pseudo-anonymity (Goodman, 2016) or quasi-anonymity (Campbell-Verduyn, 2018) that can be decrypted by law enforcement or other state agencies (see Magnuson, 2020).

As the technology evolved and as authorities obtained more knowledge about it, offenders largely abandoned bitcoin and other cryptocurrencies and these platforms have recently been assessed to carry the lowest risk for such crimes (Chowdhury, 2019). Arguments that technology *per se* is an incentive for criminal activity, thus, have little currency (as they always do). Like every new technology, blockchain and bitcoin's weaknesses in the early phases of its development have been exploited by a range of early adopters and those looking for an opportunity to engage in illicit activity. As the use of technology for offending started to decrease, the potential use of blockchain in combating crime gained traction.

Security, tracking, and crime prevention: Fighting crime, one block at the time

According to van Rijmenam and Ryan (2019), blockchain could be harnessed to prevent tax evasion and money laundering. The structure of blockchain technology, they argue, is based on trust; distributed consensus is the system's major breakthrough in this regard, as every good or bad behaviour is marked as such within the network. At any given time, every node or participant in the ledger could observe every transaction, making it almost impossible to hide or manipulate them. Further, successful and trustworthy transactions generate a higher trustworthiness rating of the nodes in the ledger. Such a model could be enhanced by adding incentive for increased transparency in the network, by improving the rating of users willing to verify their real identity with the regulator (van Rijmenam and Ryan, 2019).

The technology could also assist in tackling crimes committed outside of blockchain networks. Precluding cyber-attacks is an obvious use of DLT as decentralised systems are generally safer than centralised ones[5]. Denial of service and other attacks outlined in Chapter 4 could also be discouraged by the amount of energy and time that goes into validating blocks. Another deterrent is the fact that, if attackers want to be successful, they must alter old blocks, which again requires a great deal of computing power (Draper and Romans, 2018; Chowdhury, 2019). Providing a secure solution for sensitive laboratories, drug manufacturing industries, nuclear power plants, and other critical infrastructure establishments via blockchain technology have already been initiated in many countries around the world.

Another area of application for blockchain and DLT is in ensuring and verifying identity of things and persons, and fair trade that guarantees that producers of goods are paid fairly, working conditions are up to the standard, and that consumers get the product of a certain quality and origins (van Rijmenam and Ryan, 2019). As such, blockchain has been hailed as a potential tool that can be deployed in preventing modern slavery and human trafficking. While trafficking emerged on the international agenda more than 20 years ago (Milivojevic and Pickering, 2013), the definition of trafficking has gradually expanded over time, only to be absorbed within the broader concept of modern slavery in the 2010s (Doezema, 2010; Segrave et al., 2018; Milivojevic et al., 2020b). Modern slavery is an umbrella term for exploitative practices, including slavery, forced labour, human trafficking, debt bondage, servitude, and forced marriage (for some critical accounts of the new modern slavery framework see Chuang, 2015; O'Connell Davidson, 2015; Gallagher, 2017; Milivojevic et al., 2020b). Calls to end slavery in supply chains, however, often neglect to address local conditions, both within the community and in the labour market, that facilitate exploitation and forced labour. This lack of vision is one of the key obstacles in countering trafficking and slavery, as

> the emergence of labour brokers and subcontractors has created an environment that facilitated further lack of transparency beyond the first tier of suppliers, and an environment that is both hard to govern and investigate. The result has been low-skilled migrant workers, primarily (but not exclusively) from the Global South, being engaged in highly exploitative employment with little redress at the national level.
>
> *(Milivojevic et al., 2020a)*

Therefore, a comprehensive approach to address the issue is critical, and scholars and practitioners often turn to technology to look for answers (although with mixed results – see Milivojevic et al., 2020b: and the Special Issue of the Anti-trafficking Review, 2020, no. 14). While seeking to avoid the long line of techno-optimists that argue technology alone could be an answer for the problem, and having in mind that conditions in which trafficking and other exploitative practices thrive should not be reduced to a single cause/solution narrative, the following section looks at blockchain's promise in providing much-needed clarity and transparency for the globalised economy.

Blockchain and the supply chain governance

Supply chain management as the process of regulating and overseeing the flow of goods and services from the source to consumers includes a range of stages, depending on the industry; from producing, storing, and moving of raw materials, to producing finished goods and offering them for consumption/purchase. In a globalised world, supply chain visibility is a crucial challenge as businesses have little to no information on their second, third, or fourth-tier suppliers (Abeyratne and Monfared, 2016; Berg et al., 2020). While there are initiatives to tackle the issue and provide visualisation of end-to-end supply chains (such as Sourcemap or Mapbox), and while practices such as social ('ethical') auditing by the third party have emerged in both the Global North and Global South (Berg et al., 2020), transparency in many supply chains is still remote at best. Businesses need to opt-in and pay for these commercial products if they wish to find out the health of their supply chain. They are also getting more complex and global. These are just some reasons why tackling exploitation in supply chains is a challenging task for most businesses, especially those operating in a range of geographical settings. Consumers face similar challenges. Most often than not, we are entirely unaware of transactions and interactions our t-shirt has triggered in the past: we do not know how cotton from which the shirt is made was harvested, how much money the producer paid the workers, how was cotton transported to the manufacturing factory, who made the shirt and how much they were paid for it, and you get the point. We can find out, of course, but it takes up to a week to follow a mango from a tree to the consumer, using an existing methodology (Baucherel, 2020).

Blockchain, with its ability to instantly track every transaction, might be an essential tool in addressing these issues. The technology could provide information from the supply chain and share it with consumers at the point of sale or exchange. The shipping giant Maersk uses permissioned blockchain technology to track goods from the port to customs, providing critical transparency to stakeholders who have access to the blockchain (Baraniuk, 2020). It is also swift; it takes 2.2 seconds to map out the trail of the mango from the farm to the store using blockchain technology (Baucherel, 2020). With verification in every step of the production, delivery, and sale of products and goods, consumers have updated information about how genuine and ethical the product is. There will be no secrets hidden in supply chains: fair trade will be verifiable, and a version of a 'Greenpeace-approved' stamp Eddie and Bubble discussed in British TV comedy show *Absolutely Fabulous*[6] would mean that the product or service has been verified, and the information provided on the label confirmed by the majority, or all participants in the chain.

Significantly, this process represents a shift from a 'rescue mentality' that has long dominated anti-trafficking/slavery interventions, where those exploited were simply passive victims who need to be saved. The technology has the potential to empower migrant and other workers in precarious situations to share, map, and document work conditions and other relevant data, and in doing so, return agency and leverage to workers vulnerable to exploitation or exploited in global supply chains (Milivojevic et al., 2020b). Workers, then, become actants. Via blockchain, the role of those in precarious labour and migration situations could be pivotal: information provided by employees and their contributions in validating accuracy of data and transactions in the blockchain would be equally as important as information provided by manufacturers, transport industry, and retailers. Using blockchain, we could, consequently, contact those hard-to-reach workers and enable them to provide feedback on working conditions by verifying information in the chain, most likely using their mobile phones (as suggested by Berg et al., 2020). Yet, contrary to Berg et al. who proposed that feedback can only be fully realised when audits are deployed by businesses that have an interest and leverage to improve working conditions, blockchain is a distributed ledger not 'owned' or in any way controlled by companies or government agencies with vested interests. Its neutrality, pseudo-anonymity, structure of a distributed ledger (in which every 'node' has the copy of the ledger containing transactions), immutability, and incentivised approach to participation could bypass the governing bodies. It could also enable genuine feedback and verification by those we want to hear from. Of course, issues such as access to the Internet and technology, as well as the digital divide, are of the essence here, as technology is not accessible to everyone. The consensus protocol is also an issue, as we need to think about incentivising workers to take part in the process (see Boersma and Nolan, 2019). Moreover, blockchain might not be able to solve the 'garbage in, garbage out' problem highlighted in the previous chapters when bad entry results in bad outputs. Nevertheless, with the pace of development we see now, it is entirely plausible that new technology based on DLT or blockchain that is more accessible and simpler to use might see the light of the day in the near future. It could reach the most vulnerable and empower them in the process of labour emancipation.

From tracking goods and services in the global supply chain, blockchain's future could also be in tracking and establishing the identity of individuals. We ought to take this idea with caution, given the potential dark side of this type of globalised transparency that captures everyone, everywhere. Nevertheless, the notion that technology could be utilised for good is warranted. According to the World Bank, in 2017 there were over 1 billion people in the world who did not have an officially recognised document to prove their identity (Al-Saqaf and Seidler, 2017). These are the most vulnerable people, invisible, exploited, and abused by political regimes, businesses, and members of their own community. People also become victims of identity theft (for an example of how a heavily pregnant woman became the suspect in high profile political murder in the Middle East and other well-known cases of identity theft, see van Rijmenam and Ryan, 2019). In the US alone, 15 million people experience identity fraud and theft every year (van Rijmenam and Ryan, 2019), and our over-reliance on digital technologies and social media has certainly enhanced vulnerability to this crime. Finally, governments can often be the guilty party when it comes to denying identity and citizenship rights, as it recently happened in the UK with the 'Windrush generation' of migrants from the Commonwealth whose legal status was questioned because of a lack of accurate records (Baraniuk, 2020).

Blockchain could assist in providing necessary proofs vis-à-vis personal identity. Having identity tokens[7] embedded in the blockchain would make digital identity ID immutable, traceable, and verifiable (van Rijmenam and Ryan, 2019). The United Nations and the World Identity Network have been exploring ways to use blockchain as identity register for children as a means of combating child trafficking (United Nations, 2018; Baucherel, 2020). Refugees and asylum seekers often struggle to obtain certain rights because of lack of proof pertinent to their identity and travel. The question we need to ask here is similar to the one raised in previous chapters: is the impact of monitoring and tracking individuals via technology going to be beneficial or harmful, and which one is going to prevail?

Theorising blockchain in the future Internet: Building bridges

Blockchain has the potential to be a game-changer, not only because of its possible applications in preventing offending and victimisation; the technology provides a platform for rethinking law enforcement and crime control practices in the future Internet. Police interventions and engagements charted via AI, the IoT and mobile robots' sensors, and recorded in public or private blockchains would ensure much-needed transparency of the agency (Al-Saqaf, 2018). The application of DLT in addressing censorship, facilitating free speech, countering fake news, voting fraud, poverty, and upholding human rights is drawing attention in social sciences (van Rijmenam and Ryan, 2019; Magnuson, 2020). Blockchain could also be instrumental in addressing the Internet and other forms of government and corporate surveillance, and enforcing accountability. As indicated by van Rijmenam and Ryan (2019) and Andreas Antonopoulos (cited in Danaylov, 2016), blockchain-based innovations might be used to create a better world, not just less risky and more private financial systems. Decentralised ledgers containing data that should concern only interested parties (such as in business transactions and identity information) should remain out of the domain of governing bodies as much as possible. Amplifying security while restricting unwanted ubiquitous surveillance (including surveillance conducted by devices in the IoT networks and smart machines) is a big promise of blockchain.

It is the convergence of blockchain with other digital frontier technologies covered in this book that should be of interest for academia. Integrating technologies to achieve their best performance and address identified and potential shortcomings of DFTs is a trend in the IT industry; some examples of such integration have been presented in the previous chapters. The intersection of blockchain, AI, and the IoT is likely to shape the future Internet and 'mark a paradigm shift in our world. In fact, you cannot see these technologies as separate, as combined they will strengthen each other' (van Rijmenam and Ryan, 2019: Section 10.4 The convergence of technology). Blockchain-powered smart devices and autonomous robots will be deployed in smart homes and cities in the future (Chowdhury, 2019). Issues that might arise with the application of ambient intelligence and AI, such as violations of privacy and extensive surveillance, vulnerability to cyber-attacks, and the problem of diminishing human agency in techno-human hybrids, could be, at least to some extent, addressed by blockchain. For example, DLT could mitigate the issue of growing big data by reducing the amount shared and collected in the IoT systems by turning the systems into decentralised networks. Blockchain's privacy features secured through cryptography and semi-anonymity of participants/nodes could represent a return of privacy in contracts and transactions that have been jeopardised by oversight and surveillance of the state, corporate and financial entities. By using blockchain in the IoT systems, access to our data will be limited to those entities with public and/or a private key to the chain. By decentralising the IoT network, blockchain is likely to make the future Internet less attractive for cyberattacks and less vulnerable to a single point failure of the system. For instance, if a part of the traffic control grid in the smart city fails because of a terrorist attack, communication between members of the network could still be established via direct link based on blockchain technology. Other features of blockchain, such as immutability and distributed consensus, are of value in building more robust and less vulnerable ambient intelligence systems in smart homes and cities. As such, blockchain can assist us in achieving 'a higher level of autonomous security' (Hossain, 2020: Section 1.1: Introduction) in the future Internet.

Somewhat less clear is a potential of decentralised technology such as blockchain to reintegrate the human element in thing-human assemblages. As suggested in previous chapters, the rapid development of digital frontier technologies brings increased autonomy of things and gradual collapse of the thing-human alliance. Blockchain could be instrumental in re-establishing this connection. Other than the context of smart contracts, the technology requires an active agreement by nodes in the chain—devices and machines operated on behalf of, and by humans. Distributed consensus compels a degree of human involvement in which building the next block in the chain and maintaining the 'life' of the system needs, at least on the control level, a human oversight. However, some critics warn that blockchain might result in exactly the opposite scenario. As such, DLTs might be the final act of removal of humans from the processes about and around us, as seen in the context of smart contracts (Danaylov, 2016: Section: Andreas Antonopoulos).

Notwithstanding the above dilemma, let us go one step further in scenario writing. What if blockchain and DLT could help us solve crimes or record human right abuses? After all, AI, the IoT, and mobile robots have been used for that very purpose for years. Given that blockchain is still in its infancy, the full impact of the technology is hard to fathom. It is conceivable, however, to imagine future societies with no central authority (law enforcement or border control agency) in crime prevention and control. The network of distributed ledgers of information about objects and transactions associated with such objects could get us there without the overseeing, central authority. In the distributed, decentralised network, participants would verify transactions and events as they happen. Similar to a mango example outlined above, transactions about a 'journey' of a gun would be added to the chain. We start with the process of manufacturing a gun, followed by the transport, distribution to the seller, and the purchase of a gun by a client. But what if every next step is also added to the chain: the event (firing of a gun) and identity of a person who fired it, by bystanders and others who witnessed the crime and have access to the public ledger containing information about the incident or the gun in question? Once verified, this information becomes immutable and cannot be altered. No more tampering with evidence or police corruption. Solving crimes is a process that requires trust and a centralised organisation to get the 'truth' about what happened. By using blockchain, we could potentially get there and, at the same time, bypass crime control agencies of the state. The same process could be applied in documenting human rights abuses at the border and beyond, within immigration detention camps or in prisons.

Conclusion

Blockchain has long struggled to find the purpose beyond crypto-currencies (Baraniuk, 2020) and its future is undoubtedly one of the biggest 'unknowns' in the IT sector. As Baraniuk (2020) would have it, '[s]o far, blockchain might not have changed the world—but it has got a lot of people thinking'. There are many issues worrying experts and developers vis-à-vis blockchain and its integration with other digital frontier technologies. Possible limitations in the evolution of DLT include excessive energy needed for mining, data storage, corrupted data generated by IoT and embedded in the chain, pseudo-anonymity of nodes in blockchains, weaknesses of current consensus protocols when it comes to the timing of authentication of the transaction, and the like (for more details see Hossain, 2020). The following concerns have been flagged by social scientists: techno-credulity as a blind faith in techno-logical solutions to complex social problems such as crime, further re-moval of human agency in smart contracts, the digital divide, and the failure to reach the most vulnerable. Yet, it is critical to think about the merger of DFTs, and what impact this process might have on offending and crime control in the future Internet. Every emerging technology has its flaws. As they amalgamate some, if not most such flaws could be eliminated.

As Boersma and Nolan (2019) suggest, we cannot put all our hopes on technology as there is no such thing as a technological magic bullet that will solve our social problems, including crimes such as modern slavery and human trafficking. Blockchain and cryptocurrencies are often an example of technologies that are largely misunderstood and clouded in 'techno-fog' (Lyon, 2015). However, blockchain's promise in creating 'the good ICT society' (Bradley, 2017) and the good society more broadly—is real. In it, some sacrifices that we were supposed to make to ensure the progress of humankind might be avoided or significantly mitigated. Blockchain has the potential to create a society where the exploitation of labour might be significantly reduced, if not eliminated. This could be a society where everyone will have their unique identity and with it, fundamental human rights, and where democratic elections might be less contentious, countering AI-powered scandals such as Cambridge Analytica in the 2016 US elections. As Andreas Antonopoulous (cited in Danaylov, 2016) points out, blockchain solves the problem of anything that requires trust, without centralised organisation.

The future developments are anything but certain. As with other digital frontier technologies, obstacles and unknowns riddle the anticipated pathways for Blockchain. It is up to us to engage in scenario writing, predict the impact and consequences of DLTs, and work towards the future Internet, in which techno-social fusions will thrive yet again.

Notes

1 Whose member for a while was Julian Assange – see Magnuson (2020).
2 This is a so-called *Proof of Work* mechanism that requires powerful computers to solve complicated mathematical problems associated with blocks and uses a vast amount of energy in the process.
3 *Proof of Stake* method of achieving distributed consensus, in which the creator of the next block is chosen via the selection of wealth or age. Both shortcomings bring the idea of equality of participants in decentralised networks into question.
4 For an overview of issues pertinent to cryptomarkets and illicit drug trade, see Martin (2014).
5 In the recent COVID-19 pandemic, IT and security professionals hailed Apple and Google-developed tracking application that did not generate a copy of Bluetooth connections in a central repository as more secure than the ones that held data in centralised databases. It was suggested that decentralised ledger available on mobile phones and similar to the one in the blockchain is harder to hack and abuse, while at the same time providing enough data for health officials to track the spread of the virus. See https://www.amnesty.org.uk/press-releases/qatar-huge-security-weakness-covid-19-contact-tracing-app.
6 Edina Eddie Monsoon, played by Jennifer Saunders, is the founder and head of her own PR company. She struggles with a range of issues, from alcoholism, drug use and compulsive eating, to finding loopholes to keep her client list despite questionable work ethic and capabilities. Eddie is leaving for France and gets her personal assistant, Bubble, to do a range of tasks in absence, the key one being the refurbishment of her client Bettina's apartment. Eddie suggests that, when the wood arrives for the kitchen surfaces, Bubble should stamp it with 'Greenpeace approved' stamp, so that Bettina,

who is looking for a 'Third World Chic' look for her new kitchen, would be happy with the apparent ethical nature of the product.

7 Not the actual data about us, such as passport and social security numbers but tokens that can be related to data about us stored elsewhere, for example, the cloud or smartphone.

References

Abeyratne, S., Monfared, R., 2016. Blockchain ready manufacturing supply chain using distributed ledger. Int. J. Res. Eng. Technol. 5 (9), 1–10.

Adams, R., Kewell, B., Parry, G., 2018. Blockchain for good? digital ledger technology and sustainable development goals. In: Leal Filho, W., Marans, R.W., Callewaert, J. (Eds.), Handbook of Sustainability and Social Science Research. Springer International Publishing, Cham, pp. 127–140.

Al-Saqaf, W., 2018. Can blockchain technology improve your human rights? In: Stein, G. (Ed.), Human Rights and Blockchain. Raoul Wallenberg Institute.

Al-Saqaf, W., Seidler, N., 2017. Blockchain technology for social impact: opportunities and challenges ahead. J. Cyber Policy 2 (3), 338–354.

Baraniuk C., 2020. Blockchain: the revolution that hasn't quite happened. Available from: https://www.bbc.co.uk/news/business-51281233 (accessed 05.05.2020.).

Baucherel, K., 2020. Blockchain Hurricane: The Origins, Application, and Future of Blockchain and Cryptocurrency. Business Expert Press, New York, United States.

Berg, L., Farbenblum, B., Kintominas, A., 2020. Addressing exploitation in supply chains: is technology a game changer for worker voice? Anti-Trafficking Rev. 14, 47–66.

Boersma, M., Nolan, J., 2019. Blockchain can help break the chains of modern slavery, but it is not a complete solution. The Conversation, 2 May.

Bradley, G., 2017. The Good ICT Society: From Theory to Actions. Routledge, London, United Kingdom.

Briggs, B., Buchholz, S., Sharma, S., et al., 2019. Deloitte insights tech trends 2019: beyond the digital frontier, Deloitte. Available from: https://www2.deloitte.com/content/dam/Deloitte/br/Docu ments/technology/DI_TechTrends2019.pdf

Burks, C., 2017. Bitcoin: breaking bad or breaking barriers? N. C. J. Law Technol. 18 April.

Campbell-Verduyn, M., 2018. Bitcoin, crypto-coins, and global anti-money laundering governance. Crime Law Soc. Change 69 (2), 283–305.

Chowdhury, N., 2019. Inside Blockchain, Bitcoin, and Cryptocurrencies. Auerbach Publications, Milton, United Kingdom.

Chuang, J., 2015. The challenges and perils of reframing trafficking as 'Modern Day Slavery'. Anti-Trafficking Rev. 5, 146–149.

Danaylov, N., 2016. Conversations with the Future: 21 Visions for the 21st Century. Singularity Media Inc., Toronto.

Doezema, J., 2010. Sex Slaves and Discourse Masters: The Construction of Trafficking. Zed Books, London and New York.

Draper, T., Romans, A., 2018. Masters of Blockchain, Digital Assets and the New Capital Markets: The Rise of Cryptocurrencies, Token Economies and What That Means for Startups, Corporations and Investors. CreateSpace Independent Publishing Platform.

Gallagher, A., 2017. What is wrong with Global Slavery Index? Anti-Trafficking Rev. 8, 90–112.

Goodman, M., 2016. Future Crimes: Inside the Digital Underground and the Battle for Our Connected World. Anchor Books, New York.

Hossain, B., 2020. Critical analysis of Blockchain for Internet of Everything. In: Ahmed, M., Bakrat Ullah, A., Khan Pathan, A.-S. (Eds.), Security Analytics for the Internet of Everything. CRC Press, Bocca Ratton, London, New York.

Houben, R., Snyers, A., 2018. Cryptocurrencies and blockchain: Legal context and implications for financial crime, money laundering and tax evasion. European Parliament's Special Committee on Financial Crime, Tax Evasion and Tax Avoidance. European Parliament, Brussels.

Hulliet M., 2020. UK University Develops Blockchain Certificate to Protect Consumers from COVID-19 Risks. Available from: https://cointelegraph. com/news/uk-university-develops-blockchain-certificate-to-protect-consumers-from-covid-19-risks (accessed 27.04.2020.).

Lyon, D., 2015. Surveillance after Snowden. Polity Press, Oxford, United Kingdom.

Magnuson, W., 2020. Blockchain Democracy. Cambridge University Press, Cambridge.

Martin, J., 2014. Drugs on the Dark Net: How Cryptomarkets are Transforming the Global Trade in Illicit Drugs. Palgrave Macmillan, United Kingdom.

Milivojevic, S., Hedwards, B., Segrave, M., 2020a. Examining the promise and delivery of sustainable development goals in addressing human trafficking and modern slavery. In: Blaustein, J., Fitz-Gibbon, K., Pino, N. et al., (Eds.), Emerald Handbook on Crime, Justice and Sustainable Development. Emerald.

Milivojevic, S., Moore, H., Segrave, M., 2020b. Freeing the modern slaves, one click at a time: theorising human trafficking, modern slavery, and technology. Anti-Trafficking Rev. 14, 16–32.

Milivojevic, S., Pickering, S., 2013. Trafficking in people, 20 years on: sex, migration and crime in the global anti-trafficking discourse and the rise of the 'Global Trafficking Complex'. Curr. Issues Crim. Justice 25 (2), 585–604.

O'Connell Davidson, J., 2015. Modern Slavery: The Margins of Freedom. Palgrave Macmillan, London.

Reijers, W., Coeckelbergh, M., 2018. The blockchain as a narrative technology: investigating the social ontology and normative configurations of crypto-currencies. Philos. Technol. 31 (1), 103–130.

Segrave, M., Milivojevic, S., Pickering, S., 2018. Sex Trafficking and Modern Slavery: The Absence of Evidence. Routledge, London and New York.

Tvede, L., 2020. Supertrends: 50 Things You Need to Know about the Future. John Wiley & Sons, Incorporated, Newark.

United Nations. 2018. World Economic and Social Survey 2018: Frontier technologies for sustainable development. United Nations Department of Economic and Social Affairs, New York.

van Rijmenam, M., Ryan, P., 2019. Blockchain: Transforming Your Business and Our World. Routledge, London and New York.

van Wegberg, R., Oerlemans, J.-J., van Deventer, O., 2018. Bitcoin money laundering: mixed results? An explorative study on money laundering of cybercrime proceeds using bitcoin. J. Financ. Crime 25 (2), 419–435.

Wintermeyer, L., 2019. Blockchain at the united nations leading solutions to the global crisis. Forbes, 26 September. https://www.forbes.com/sites/lawrencewintermeyer/2019/09/26/blockchain-at-the-united-nations-leading-solutions-to-the-global-crisis/

7

INSTEAD OF CONCLUSION

Criminology's take on digital frontier technologies

Deciphering digital frontier technologies

Societies have long been defined by technology. Yet, the pace and magnitude of the technological growth in the late twentieth and twenty-first century are poised to fundamentally alter the way we live, work, entertain, consume, and socialise. The apparent permanent state of flux of emerging technologies brings many challenges we need to respond to, but the pressing question is: where do we start? How can we begin to engage with the future in a meaningful and productive way, given how uncertain the future is, and given that we do not know if or when technologies covered in this book (or other emerging technologies such as quantum computing, for example) are going to 'cross the chasm' and become mainstream? We do not know whether AGI or level 5 automation for mobile robots is going to occur soon, or at all. We are also in the dark about what is going to happen when technologies merge. What we do know, however, is that artefacts of the Fourth Industrial Revolution have a significant impact on our lives. We modify our behaviour and adopt technological innovations because they are marketed as an improvement of our life and skills, or because they are irresistible or necessary, and for many other reasons outlined in this book and elsewhere. Life 3.0 might be just around the corner. In it, both hardware and software will be 'upgradable', at least to some extent. Things, devices, and machines around us will continue to multiply and become smarter.

They will be even more connected, communicating with one another and gaining new skills and capabilities through such connections. Code, things and machines' communication networks are likely to become decentralised and entirely automated. Smart algorithms will generate action on our behalf, often without our knowledge or approval. They will be increasingly independent in reaching set goals or establishing new ones without our input or awareness. As Weiser (1991: 94) suggests, '[t] he most profound technologies are those that disappear. They weave themselves into the fabric of everyday life until they are indistinguishable from it'. Even if we manage to comprehend these processes, we might not opt-out. In the future Internet, humans will be both optimistic and have great fears. Digital frontier technologies bring techno-credulity and anxiety around catastrophic risks that are prominent in times of crisis (such as the 2020 COVID-19 epidemic), while our engagement with such advancements remains limited at best.

This book had the following overarching goal: to map the origins and current and future developments of digital frontier technologies, their interactions with crime and criminal justice, and impending impact on a range of social actors and communities. Its starting premise was that while we cannot be sure where technology is heading, we need to engage with critical innovations so that we mitigate, if not eliminate, some of its unwanted consequences. This premise was underpinned by a notion that, in the twenty-first century, the importance of technological artefacts is so critical that we could no longer think about the future without positioning smart things and algorithms in the centre of our analysis. Things around us have long gained agency. While they might never obtain intention or consciousness, agency of non-humans demonstrated in obtaining set or self-imposed goals leads to many, sometimes even life-altering outcomes for individuals and communities. Algorithms, smart devices, and machines are drivers of technological, social, and political change. Having this in mind, the book adopted a post-humanist approach, looking at agency distributed amongst all actors in techno-human assemblages. Critical agents, human or not, were scrutinised and analysed, as was their individual and co-agency. A concern raised in the previous chapters was that human agency is becoming less critical and that the equilibrium between humans and our hi-tech companion species is in jeopardy.

Homo sapiens, whether willingly or unwillingly, increasingly find themselves at the fringes of decision-making and engagement in many areas of social interactions. Thing-to-thing communications and collaborations are growing, both in terms of size and impact. Big data about our habits, health, fitness, consumer practices, travel, and love life are generated, analysed, and acted upon by algorithms, smart devices, and machines every second of our existence. While we sometimes volunteer information to these growing databases, data about us is often automated, augmented, and processed by smart things. Certainly, this is not necessarily, or not always, a bad thing. Algorithmic decision-making in many areas of our life—work, health, travel, and the like—has been heralded by many as bias-free and supreme. There is no doubt that smart things could perform many tasks better than we ever could. Limitations of humans when it comes to choosing the best route for travel or the best candidate for the job are seemingly bypassed by impartial, perpetual 'gaze' and 'brain' of smart algorithms. They also replace us in performing hazardous tasks and hard labour. However, in the pursuit of security and a better, healthier, and more comfortable life, other, more critical human inputs are likely to be reduced. As this book has demonstrated, some decisions should not be left to devices and machines—well, at least not exclusively, without human oversight and input.

Moreover, our privacy will be irrevocably changed. Security framing of frontier technologies is well underway, with necessary 'trade-offs' made for the greater good of the majority. Our lives are becoming more transparent, tangled in the networks of 'surveillant assemblages'. Those marginalised are over-surveilled and further discriminated against, but we are all under its gaze. Importantly, human actors stay disengaged, scarcely challenging the context and practices of ubiquitous surveillance. Technology slowly sinks into the unconscious, as we become obedient to artefacts and algorithms, quietly accepting our faith and their decisions made on our behalf. On the other hand, the potential of technology to empower and safeguard privacy, limit surveillance, and promote a more egalitarian, democratic, and just society, as demonstrated in Chapter 6, should not be underestimated or overlooked.

Crime and punishment in the future Internet: State of the affairs and possible trajectories

To regain some control over the development of technology and its impact, and propose legislative, policy, and technological interventions to follow such processes, we must analyse and theorise DFTs. We ought to start with available tools and frameworks and build new ones as we go. In *Crime and Punishment in the Future Internet*, I began by applying a range of relevant theories from various disciplines to DFTs. Of course, the list is not definitive. I invite you to leave feedback and comments on the book's companion website (www.crimetechbook.com) with ideas and suggestions to enrich these and further theoretical inquiries on the topic. In the previous chapters, ANT was utilised to identify the human and non-human source of action in the future Internet. Humans and our companion species were supposed to mutually control our social inter-actions. Yet, we see instances of *blackboxing* in everyday applications of digital frontier technologies. Non-human mediators that do not translate input into a defined output but have an element of surprise and un-certainty are gaining traction and altering social fabric and relationships. Their growing cooperation, aimed at reaching mutual or individual goals, might lead to a scenario where goals of smart things might not be aligned with ours. Digital life of our companion species might increas-ingly be out of our control and oversight, all the while our existence is being stripped naked, under the watchful eye of our little helpers, mobile robots, and smart algorithms. We will all be targets, but many groups and individuals will feel the impact of this process disproportionately.

A potential impact of DFTs on offending, victimisation, crime pre-vention, and penal policies and practices is difficult to predict but should not be dismissed. In this first examination of emerging technologies and their complex relationships with criminology, conclusions should not and cannot be drawn. As it was demonstrated in previous chapters, AI, the IoT, autonomous mobile robots, and blockchain have already begun to fundamentally alter how crimes are committed, solved, administered, and punished. One of the questions posed in this book is should AI be subject to criminal law and criminally liable, or should our focus be on humans—coders and users. This dilemma should be read and analysed within a broader logic of Catch-22: shall we adopt the human-centric or post-human approach when it comes to technology? Given the stand-point adopted in this book was that the thing-human alliance is critical for understanding crime and offending in the future Internet, it was suggested that we ought to think outside the box and consider direct liability in some instances. If AI and AI-powered mobile robots and the IoT systems act as mediators and create 'emergence', in which AI acts beyond originally intended ways, wouldn't this approach be the most appropriate one? This is a topic for future criminological research, in partnerships with legal scholars and experts. The book also raises many other matters pertinent to offending with the assistance of, or performed by, DFTs. Of course, as it was to be expected in a book that is the first examination of an issue, I could not offer more than a brief overview of pressing contemporary issues, those identified as such by experts and commentators (and by me, using scanning and scenario writing methods). Other applications of emerging technologies in offending are likely, and as such, need to be investigated in the future. One such example is the use of AI and the IoT in stalking and family violence.

Digital frontier technologies have been changing government agencies' efforts to prevent (or rather foresee) criminal behaviour, assist in criminal proceedings, and overall change our engagement with issues around policing and victimisation. Many such examples have been outlined in this volume: from HunchLab, VALCRI, facial recognition machine learning applications, detection, and investigation of traffic offences and 'remote control' policing, investigation of online fraud, to child sex offences, human trafficking, and modern slavery. The potential of blockchain to 'map' offending presented in Chapter 6 might look a bit far-fetched. However, such scenarios require further exploration. Technological artefacts could, arguably, abolish certain types of criminality, as well as the need for discretionary policing practices. One illustration offered in the book is traffic offences and autonomous cars. This development could be particularly important for groups disproportionately targeted by police, such as racial and ethnic minorities. The technology could also address some misuses of other DFTs, such as the use of blockchain in stopping cyber and DDoS attacks in smart cities of the future. Emerging technologies could also save lives and prevent suffering, as witnessed in the debate on humanitarian drones. They could assist us in abandoning 'rescue mentality' and return leverage and agency to those impacted by globalisation-induced crimes and injustices.

Policing in the future Internet is likely to look somewhat different, with more actors involved in the security industry (as demonstrated in the case of mobile robots such as K5, or via distributed ledger technology). Whether or not these technological advancements are going to eliminate the need for over-policing, and how the police are going to respond to challenges prompted by its use (such as, for example, deployment of drones for public disturbances and offending, or autonomous swarm drones patrolling 'roborder' that could tap into portable 'smart things' to determine whether you are legitimate border crosser or not as debated in Chapter 5), is anyone's guess. Are we going to witness a new dawn of police powers? Is law enforcement going to be delegated to other actors and consumers? We do not have answers to such queries right now. The change is ongoing and fast, and we need to monitor, research, analyse, predict, and influence its development as much as possible. Courtrooms will change as well. Ambient intelligence has been increasingly used in criminal proceedings where our little helpers routinely testify against us. In the smart cities of the future, we are likely to see more technological innovations employed for this very purpose, and we should not outright dismiss such advances.

At the same time, new types of pervasive and hard-to-opt-out-of surveillance at the border and beyond have been deployed. The goal of such interventions is to obtain information about who we are and where we are at all times. 'Dronisation' of borders is one example outlined in this volume that illustrates this process. Keeping humans deemed risky and dangerous (illegalised border crossers, potential offenders, and recidivists) at arm's length is the pinnacle of such interventions. Privacy violations, algorithmic governance, self-imposed regulatory behaviours are mechanisms to do just that. Data, it is argued, does not lie; it is objective and accurate. We need to learn to unpack the truth and foresee future offending as predicted by smart algorithms. Actuarial justice as the process of identifying and managing people according to risk before they commit a crime has found a new ground in AI. Pre-crime narratives call for increasingly earlier interventions not by creating fewer opportunities for offending, but by 'predicting'—using machine learning algorithms—the crime scene, and prospective wrongdoers. Emerging technologies move us further away from analysing past patterns of crime and deviance to predicting the future. Threats and risks (of offending, deviant behaviour, violations of border and migration regimes, and the like) are deemed as calculable, foreseeable, and inevitable even though they are none of these things. Predictive policing based on crime and non-crime related data that is likely to include information from social media platforms or ambient intelligence is hailed as scientific, credible, and revolutionary. Identifying places and people linked to future crimes is not in the realm of science fiction anymore. Fuelled by biased information fed into these systems, non-transparent, non-accurate, and highly lucrative crime-predicting applications not only make up data about crime and offending; they increasingly remove humans from such processes. PredPol 4.0 is likely to be harmful to many, and we cannot underestimate its potential detrimental effects. Machine learning underpinned smart things will 'disrupt' crime and 'pre-empt' offending by arresting, prosecuting, adjudicating, and sentencing people for crimes they may never commit. They could turn into super-detectives and judges that punish intent, or simply 'wrong' associations—being in the wrong place at the wrong time, of a certain race, class, or else. They will be heralded as objective, and decisions things make will be final, irrevocable, and almost impossible to contest. We are unlikely to understand how algorithms come to such verdicts but will trust their objectivity. This *blackboxing* potential of DFTs is one of the key concerns raised in this volume. The more successful smart things become, the opaquer they will be for consumers and experts. With apparent consequences that impede on human rights and civil liberties, removal of human agency accompanied by a lack of safeguards that will ensure a fair and transparent criminal justice process is the path we must avoid.

So, how should we regulate or reverse these developments? Some suggestions were made in this volume, such as the adoption of the Model of Care (Asaro, 2019) approach in AI and the implementation of Asimov's Three Laws of Robotics or an 'updated' version of rules that would acknowledge intricacies of human-thing assemblages. Rather than working on technology that aims to identify and prevent risks and threats, we should aspire to develop technology that attains values and goals that would benefit everyone. This process is not merely revaluing qualitative vs. quantitative data. Artificial intelligence and other emerging technologies should be built to learn, adopt, and retain our goals. Issues around crime, victimisation, crime prevention, recidivism, and penal policies are so complex and nonlinear; as such, they cannot be solved by the binary approach of risk/threat vs. non-risk/non-threat. Using some digital frontier technologies can address limitations of others: blockchain's potential in addressing concerns around privacy and surveillance brought by the development of AI and the IoT, but also serious crimes such as labour exploitation, human trafficking, and modern slavery require close inspection. Finally, more data about the social does not automatically translate into better solutions; yet, it can certainly help in finding such solutions. It is what we do with data that matters. AI, autonomous mobile robots, the IoT, and blockchain have the potential to assist us in understanding why people offend, how we can implement better crime prevention strategies, and to better address underlying contexts that enable offending such as poverty, unemployment, discrimination, homelessness, lack of education, and the like. This approach is expected to yield more tangible and long-lasting results than the ones that focus on using technology to 'predict' what humans (or machines, for that matter) might do in the future.

Where to go from here?

While acknowledging the standpoint of Luddites, sceptics, and techno-utopians in this book, I adopted the stance of beneficial AI that looks at how to harvest existing and forthcoming technology for good. I am not suggesting that other philosophical frameworks are less relevant or erroneous. *A contrario*, such perspectives can be, and often are both comprehensible and theoretically and morally sound. I simply believe this position enables us to constructively engage with what is known as a 'control problem' and the impact of unsupervised agency of technological artefacts. One example of this is the process of reproducing and reinforcing bias via technology, a topic explored at length in this volume. The sections on automated profiling and crime forecasting (Chapter 3), as well as policing in the era of smart mobile machines (Chapter 5), detail many conundrums pertinent to 'neutrality' of technology. I also looked at how some of the concerns regarding the renaissance and shortcomings of actuarial justice could be addressed in the future Internet. Thus, the question we should focus on is whether we could develop technology that is likely to eradicate, rather than reinforce, bias. This question is critical as '[t]he challenges of the future are rarely solved with the technologies of today' (Tvede, 2020: Section Our knowledge at double speed, subsection 4). Addressing censorship, ubiquitous surveillance, and human rights violations, while at the same time facilitating free speech, democratic practices, transparency, accountability, and the rule of law should not only be the task for humans. We need to find creative, inventive ways to reconcile our values with technology, and harness technology to help us build a better world. The crucial thing, however, is to cease to be passive observers. Whether early adopters or experts, we need to be prepared, as much as possible, for what is to come. In doing so, we need to bypass boundaries: disciplinary, physical, and national. Installing fundamental values in DFTs and deploying precautions requires action and creative and innovative thinking, as well as novel frameworks. The claim that big data and emerging technologies might signal the end of theorising crime and offending is fundamentally flawed and can lead to more *blackboxing* (for more on this, see Chan and Bennett Moses, 2016).

Foresight approach, as well as other methodological tools (such as backcasting that defines a desirable future and identifies steps and policies we need to put in place to get there), enable meaningful engagement with technology in and across a range of disciplines. By looking at the current state of technological expansion and envisioning multiple pictures of the future—however implausible and unlikely they currently appear—we could potentially mitigate or eliminate some negative consequences of the Fourth Technological Revolution. This intervention is critical for everyone: developers, early adopters, consumers, business people, politicians, academics, community workers, health professionals, policy makers, residents of smart cities, and border crossers.

The following areas of urgent concern for criminologists and social science researchers, in conjunction with our STEM colleagues, are (in no particular order):

• Addressing techno-fog/*blackboxing* and ensuring transparency
  Digital frontier technologies are yet another example of progress engulfed by lack of transparency and understanding of how technology works. While we continue to use increasingly complex AI-powered smart devices and autonomous mobile robots for a range of daily chores and purposes, and as we begin to implant such technology into our bodies, we seem to know less about how things operate, communicate, make decisions, and create and achieve goals. Just pause for a second and reflect on your knowledge of your surroundings, technology you use at home, workplace, or in a car, or reflect on some examples used in this book. How much do you know about how smart home devices, or semi-autonomous cars, work? As Carl Sagan (cited in Goodman, 2016: 466) warns, '[w]e might get away with it for a while, but sooner or later this combustible mixture of ignorance and power is going to blow up in our faces'. This ignorance is particularly dangerous given that we live in times where '[n]ever have so many people had so much access to so much knowledge and yet have been so resistant to learning anything' (Nichols, 2017: 2).
  Certainly, we appreciate that technology can assist us in a range of daily tasks and can make our everyday life and experiences more pleasant and enjoyable. Our health has also been improved by technology. Nevertheless, we need a greater understanding of both current contexts and future trajectories and possible scenarios. To be clear, I am not referring only to end-users here; experts will soon struggle to comprehend the details of technology too. Advances in AI are of concern; as indicated at the beginning of this book, significantly more effort and money have been put in advancing technology, rather than understanding and addressing its shortcomings and pursuing 'explainable AI' that would provide answers to how systems make decisions and why. This lack of focus is particularly worrying given that smart things and code have been—and will increasingly be—making decisions about our rights and liberties. Decisions on punishment, sentence, bail, parole, and chances of

recidivism are likely to be even more non-transparent, beyond question, oversight, and scrutiny. This is both dangerous and un-acceptable for citizens and non-citizens in the Global North and the Global South.

Imposing bans on features of technology in order to prevent misuse and offending (as suggested in addressing shortcomings of blockchain in Chapter 6), or banning technology altogether, is another *cul-de-sac*. I am aware that many experts and readers will disagree, for ex-ample, when it comes to the use of facial recognition and AI in policing. My main argument here is that bans are unlikely to yield the results we desire. What we need instead is more time, effort, and energy invested in anticipating and assessing the negative impact of existing and future innovations. Undoubtedly, with technological advances, many obstacles are likely to emerge, especially in its early stages of maturity. Some technologies are going to disappear, while others emerge. As such, the most critical thing in mapping our future engagement with technology in the context of social sciences is not only unpacking the ins and outs of that particular innovation. It is essential to think about how we relate to the innovation, and what can be done with it. We need to think about smart things as our companion species and act accordingly.

- Strong AI, ethics, and privacy by design

In this book, I deliberately avoided the debate around AGI, while I did engage with the question of the morality of technology. This decision is somewhat controversial as the two issues are intertwined. Technology has moral relevance, and this issue will be even more pressing as machine learning and DFTs evolve. Researchers should endeavour to engage with both issues as they are critical for addressing and mitigating the impact of technology on offending, victimisation, and criminal justice interventions. As discussed at length in the next point, we need to make sure technology is not used for human rights violations and encroaching civil liberties, and that specific ethics codes are embedded into technology. As one of my computer science friends suggested, we might even need Chief Ethical Intelligence Officers that would operate in a range of business and government settings. Yet, just which trajectory we ought to follow is less certain. As demonstrated in Chapter 5, there is no agreement among experts, coders, and other stakeholders around which strategy to adopt when it comes to ethics in smart machines: preference, equality, or neutrality. This is another issue that warrants a debate, and if possible, a resolution.

We need to further the conversation by looking into standards that will guide the advances of these and other emerging technologies. Harnessing technology for good, while steering clear from false promises, needs to be at the forefront of research in STEM and social sciences. In doing so, we need to implement privacy by design approach and consider how we can utilise existing technologies, such as blockchain, that could address privacy intrusions and other shortcomings of DFTs. Privacy is likely to change, but the notion that privacy is the thing of the past needs to be reconsidered, if not contested. Implementing ethical principles into smart things is not the only branch of ethics academia should focus on. It is equally important to make sure that we discuss the moral dimensions of human-to-thing and thing-to-thing associations with people building and designing technology, as well as early adopters and other end users. This approach is complementary to our greater understanding of the ins and outs of technological innovations, as we should focus on how the technology works and how to use it for good.

• Identifying, alleviating, and preventing harm and discrimination
Advances in technology do not necesserily translate into a better, more equal world. While this book has only sporadically addressed matters such as the use of DFTs in a war, or designing technology to harm people, these are important issues to discuss in the future. Dilemmas raised by the use and justification of designing autonomous mobile robots for the primary purpose of killing human beings should worry us all. However, so-called 'civilian' use of technology is often harmful too, as witnessed in the context of border control. Drone stare and mechanical distance used to dehumanise and disrupt unwanted and unauthorised mobility is just one example that illustrates how complex and manifold harm that accompanies technology can be. Even when technology *per se* is not harmful, it might be prone to hacks and misuse. What is needed is a clear understanding of mistakes in current and future paths of technological development, and what—if any—'collateral damage' we are willing to tolerate. Outlining harm and human cost, often hidden behind benevolent technology narrative, ought to be a priority.
Robust legal frameworks that will identify and anticipate harms created by techno-social fusions, especially AI and machine learning technology, are critical for our future engagement with smart things. The vulnerability of artefacts and code, not just in relation to hacks and intrusions but also their actions as actants, decision-makers, and goal

setters (especially goals that might not align with humans') must be at the forefront of future research and policymaking. Even if we do not believe that 'crime harvest' is going to happen with the growth of the IoT and autonomous mobile robots, and if we dismiss the claim that the growth of ambient intelligence and AI-powered devices is a security disaster waiting to happen, the reach of smart things that might soon be implanted into our body requires careful consideration. 'Mission creep', where technology will serve not only to combat crime but those identified as unwanted or inherently deviant (such as illegalised border crossers and racial minorities), need to be prevented and/or disrupted. The current and future use of the IoT and mobile robots for border security under the guise of 'saving lives', while such practices create seamless borders, is a narrative that needs to be deconstructed.

- The commercialisation of digital frontier technologies
The money question is a critical issue that has not been explored in this volume. The reason for this omission is that I thought I could not do it justice in a short volume such as this book. This absence is a limitation as many experts, including leading scholars who reviewed this volume such as Professor Dean Wilson, consider this issue the most important in the technology-crime nexus. Technological artifacts, Professor Wilson suggests, might be an avenue by which capitalism spreads deeper into our everyday lives. Indeed, many technological advances discussed here might no longer serve the intended purpose (for good) and are not needed or wanted by consumers; however, they are imposed on us and marketed as inevitable. This concern is both legitimate and real, and as such, requires our attention.

Commercialisation currently drives much of big data and AI work; the narrative of advertising and selling things intersects with privacy and civil liberties and as such requires unequivocal consideration. We have seen a range of negative consequences of the privatisation of the prison-industrial complex and is reasonable to expect similar scenarios here. There is little transparency about how private companies sell their 'crime prevention' and security products (software and/or hardware) to governments and consumers. An issue linked to this is who controls and has access to our data. These could be the starting points in our investigation of commercialisation of DFTs and how such processes impact on practices and strategies of crime control.

- Bringing human back to the human–thing alliance
The decision ought to be made on whether we need to harness technology to bring human agency back to the fore. There is a clear

need for a public and scientific debate about this issue before we continue to develop technologies that further remove us from the equation. We cannot allow to find ourselves in a situation where turning off devices and machines amounts to our suicide. Irrelevance of humanity in the world of connected, learning things and machines is a reason for trepidation. Alternatively, maybe we should see ourselves as poets and artists of the past; as labour as we know it today will be delegated to things, while humans intellectualise and contemplate our existence, nature, and the future. Whatever scenario we pursue, well-defined human-thing protocols must be implemented, in which our place in the future Internet will be outlined with clarity and consensus. As Papacharissi (2019: Section 1, Introduction, para. 1) would have it, '[i]nevitably, the dreams and nightmares rendered by the limits of our human imagination revolve around the same theme: will technology fundamentally alter the essence of what it means to be human? And the answer, despite the countless narratives of anticipation and apprehension is, I find, the same: only if we permit it to do so'. I could not agree more.

Thus, it is time to join forces in scenario writing and plan future research, explore options and trajectories, predict the impact and consequences of approaching innovations, theorise using existing but also innovative frameworks, and lead the way in exploring and designing responses to offending and victimisation in the future Internet.

References

Asaro, P., 2019. AI ethics in predictive policing: from models of threat to ethics of care. IEEE Technol. Soc. Mag. 38 (2), 40–53.

Chan, J., Bennett Moses, L., 2016. Is big data challenging criminology? Theor. Criminol. 20 (1), 21–39.

Goodman, M., 2016. Future Crimes: Inside the Digital Underground and the Battle for Our Connected World. Anchor Books, New York.

Nichols, T., 2017. The Death of Expertise: The Campaign against Established Knowledge and Why it Matters. Oxford University Press, Oxford.

Papacharissi, Z., 2019. Introduction. In: Papacharissi, Z. (Ed.), A Neworked Self and Human Augmentics, Artificial Intelligence, Sentience. Routledge, London and New York.

Tvede, L., 2020. Supertrends: 50 Things You Need to Know about the Future. John Wiley & Sons, Incorporated, Newark.

Weiser, M., 1991. The computer for the 21st century. Sci. Am. 265 (3), 94–105.

INDEX

For Product Safety Concerns and Information please contact our EU
representative GPSR@taylorandfrancis.com
Taylor & Francis Verlag GmbH, Kaufingerstraße 24, 80331 München, Germany

www.ingramcontent.com/pod-product-compliance
Lightning Source LLC
Chambersburg PA
CBHW071207050326
40689CB00011B/2268

* 9 7 8 0 3 6 7 4 6 8 0 0 2 *